Growing Leaders Within

Growing Leaders Within

A Process toward Teacher Leadership

Michael Coquyt and Brian Creasman

ROWMAN & LITTLEFIELD
Lanham • Boulder • New York • London

Published by Rowman & Littlefield
A wholly owned subsidiary of The Rowman & Littlefield Publishing Group, Inc.
4501 Forbes Boulevard, Suite 200, Lanham, Maryland 20706
www.rowman.com

Unit A, Whitacre Mews, 26-34 Stannary Street, London SE11 4AB

British Library Cataloguing in Publication Information Available

Library of Congress Cataloging-in-Publication Data

Names: Creasman, Brian, author. | Coquyt, Michael, author.
Title: Growing leaders within : a process toward teacher leadership / Brian Creasman and Michael Coquyt.
Description: Lanham : Rowman & Littlefield, 2017. | Includes bibliographical references and index.
Identifiers: LCCN 2017020045 (print) | LCCN 2017024542 (ebook) | ISBN 9781475838060 (electronic) | ISBN 9781475838046 (hardcover : alk. paper) | ISBN 9781475838053 (paperback)
Subjects: LCSH: Teacher participation in administration. | Teachers—Professional relationships. | School improvement programs. | Educational leadership.
Classification: LCC LB2806.45 (ebook) | LCC LB2806.45 .C74 2017 (print) | DDC 371.2—dc23
LC record available at https://lccn.loc.gov/2017020045

∞™ The paper used in this publication meets the minimum requirements of American National Standard for Information Sciences Permanence of Paper for Printed Library Materials, ANSI/NISO Z39.48-1992.

Printed in the United States of America

Contents

Foreword

> The task of leadership is not to put greatness into humanity, but to elicit it, for the greatness is already there.

This quote by novelist and historian John Buchan resonates with my personal leadership vision of helping school administrators discover their greatness within. The best leaders deliberately grow and empower others for extraordinary outcomes.

Growing Leaders Within: A Process toward Teacher Leadership takes this concept from Buchan and provides a step-by-step guide to develop teacher leaders—a force for improving the whole school. The book is based on research from hundreds of school administrators who are successful in growing teacher leaders in 24 states throughout the nation and Australia.

Authors Michael Coquyt, Ed.D., and Brian Creasman, Ed.D., are practitioners who turn insight into action. Both have extensive and wide-ranging careers in public education and are sought after for their input when it comes to teacher leadership. Individually and collaboratively, Michael and Brian have a long history of successfully growing teacher leaders both in the K–12 and postsecondary settings.

When it comes to student success, the learning fates of principals, teachers, and students are interconnected. Teacher leaders serve as a lynchpin to remarkable growth in student achievement. They are committed to the school and students' long-term success. Equally as important, teacher leaders support the role of principals ensuring they are exemplary leaders who lead schools of the future.

I applaud you for exploring this book and seeking information. It is filled with clear strategy for growing teacher leaders, as well as skill development and growth opportunities to ensure you elicit the greatness within your teachers and the students you serve.

Rhonda Caldwell, CAE, Ed.D.
Deputy Director of the Kentucky Association of School Administrators
and
Director of the Center for Education Leadership

Preface

PURPOSE OF BOOK

The impulse to write this book began soon after the completion of our first, *The Leader Within*. We looked on that work as foundational in the sense that if anyone wanted to know more about teacher leadership or the Teacher Leader Model Standards (TLMS), reading the book could be an option. *The Leader Within* wasn't written for a particular audience. We both use it as a text in our graduate courses, and it has been well received by our students and administrators and teachers who have read it. *Growing Leaders Within* grew, for lack of a better term, from questions we received about teacher leadership, from our previous work, and from our own curiosity.

Growing Leaders Within is purposefully written in a pragmatic manner and is written for a specific audience, school administrators. We make mention of *The Leader Within* numerous times in this book for good reason. To develop teacher leaders and grow a collaborative leadership culture, you need to know a thing or two about teacher leadership. In our humble opinion, *The Leader Within* is a good place to start. After acquiring knowledge about teacher leadership, we believe the next logical step is exercising that knowledge. We both received numerous questions from administrators about the book and the standards, but the most common question was "How can I use this information?" This is the point where our curiosity kicked in.

Full disclosure, although we both have experience working with, developing, and empowering teacher leaders, we didn't necessarily use the TLMS. We did employ some semblance of the standards, but it wasn't until we researched and wrote *The Leader Within* that we became thoroughly aware of how they could be used in schools. This is similar to a veteran teacher who uses differentiated instruction to meet the diverse needs of his or her students, without even knowing it. Excellent teachers just do it without realizing it. This isn't to say that we were both excellent administrators, far from it. But, we both understood collaborative leadership and had extraordinary teachers who we could count on to execute and carry out certain tasks.

The second-most common question about teacher leadership that we have received is, "What does this look like in schools?" Initially, we both fell back on our experience growing teacher leaders and started putting together a blueprint or template for how this might look. In researching this topic we came across some fascinating work about teacher leaders including that done by Crowther and colleagues (2009) and Levin and Schrum (2017). As a former (4 years removed) and current administrator, we appreciate how busy and complicated the typical school work week can be.

We both have firsthand knowledge how busy administrators are today and the last thing they need is something that is going to take up their most valuable commodity, time. We understood that any new "program" would need to fit into the normal, day-to-day operations of both teacher and administrator. We contend that *Growing Leaders Within* is different from previous works about teacher leadership because of its pragmatic nature, its use of the TLMS as a conceptual framework, and maybe most important, our process is doable in today's educational settings.

Our conversations about growing teacher leaders began to take shape in the summer of 2016. By that time we had done the research, put together a framework for growing teacher leaders that seemed feasible, but were curious about what is currently being done in schools to grow teacher leaders. We decided to survey as many administrators as we could about the processes they used to grow teacher leaders in their schools/districts. We came up with three different versions of the teacher–leader survey (Appendix A) and randomly sent them out. Each survey examines teacher leadership from a slightly different perspective. All told, more than 10,000 surveys were dispatched. We did our best to target only those administrators who had experience working with teacher leaders.

We received hundreds of responses from 24 states including Australia. Anyone who has performed qualitative research using survey questions understands how time-consuming this process can be. It was time-consuming, but at the same time, exhilarating. We had a stipulation in our methodology about the use of follow-up interviews if some of our responses weren't specific enough. A number of our respondents were interviewed again, and soon thereafter explicit themes began to emerge. The responses we received, along with the TLMS, shape and inform the foundation of our seven-phase process for growing teacher leaders.

In the end, what started out as conversations about growing teacher leaders has produced a book devoted to growing the most precious resource administrators have, their teachers. The reader will soon find out that the first three phases can be accomplished not by doing more, but rather, by realizing, recognizing, and thinking about whom might fit the mold of a teacher leader. The next two phases can be accomplished by using existing groups and committees. The real work for the administrator comes with their providing professional growth opportunities for your teacher leaders. This will require a time commitment, but our re-

search and our experience has taught us that most administrators actually enjoy reflecting, discussing, and working on true "leadership" activities.

Acknowledgments

To the Experienced or Aspiring School Administrator and Teacher Leader:

We want to recognize and applaud the work that you do each day to make our schools the best for students. We realize that schools are complex organizations and your dedication to the field of education is truly inspiring. Teaching tomorrow's future remains the noblest profession that exists in today's society. Without teachers, we recognize that we would not be able to write this book, and we thank you for serving and leading.

After the success of our first book, *The Leader Within*, many authors might have stopped writing; however, we realized that our teacher leadership journey had only begun. It was meant to be a foundational work: a practical look at teacher leadership through the Teacher Leader Model Standards (2012) lens. As schools continue to grow in complexities, we offer *Growing Leaders Within* as tool and resource to assist you in growing a culture of teacher leadership in your school.

Time and time again, we are asked about what the process of growing teacher leaders looks like in schools. As a result, we provide this book as a basis to help you begin the journey toward growing teacher leaders. Our research-based process will help you to identify, encourage, and develop others to reach their fullest potential as a teacher leader.

Similar to our previous endeavors we appreciate that the study of teacher leadership is not new; however, the actual practice of growing and developing teacher leaders is. The void in the current literature about teacher leadership that we hope this book satisfies is twofold. First, the process of growing teacher leaders can be done in conjunction with many of the duties that you are already performing as an administrator. Second, we offer our insights about professional development specific for teacher leaders.

We are grateful for the support, help, and assistance of many people. First, we want to thank all school principals, district administrators, and superintendents who participated in the research study that provided the basis for *Growing Leaders Within*. Your contributions have been invaluable and will help others who begin the process to growing teacher leaders.

We have been fortunate to work with a phenomenal and talented editorial and production team at Rowman and Littlefield for a second time. Tom Koerner, who has become a mentor for us and continues to believe in our work and our vision. We also want to thank Emily Tuttle who has helped us to navigate the publishing process and continues to provide invaluable feedback to make this book better.

A special thanks goes out to Dr. Rhonda Caldwell who wrote the perfect foreword to *Growing Leaders Within,* her dedication to the area of school leadership development and support continues to go unmatched. Her expertise in the area of leadership development continues to grow nationally and we are fortunate to call her a colleague, mentor, and friend. In addition, we want to thank our colleagues who reviewed our manuscript early on.

We are fortunate and honored to have the support and endorsements from Dr. Keith Ballard, Dr. Lu Young, Dr. Paul Borthwick, and Dr. Steven Miletto. The four of them individually continue to be national leaders in education and a voice for students and teacher leadership, which only makes their endorsements more special. They truly are among the best in the business, and their wealth of knowledge about teacher leadership inspires us to continue to pursue understanding how to empower teachers to be leaders.

Most importantly, we are tremendously grateful to our families for supporting, encouraging, and inspiring us to continue to write about teacher leadership. They, more than anyone else, have come to understand how important this subject is to both of us. We thank them in advance as we continue to explore and research a topic that has become a main part of our professional lives over the past several years.

Introduction

HOW THE BOOK IS ORGANIZED

Much like our previous work *The Leader Within*, the goal of this book is to remain simple to read, understand, and use. Though educators will be the primary users of the book, we find that it is important not to include what is referred to as "educational jargon" but instead offer clear and useful strategies for growing teacher leaders. The book is simplistic in organization and presentation.

The first six chapters will follow the same sequence explained here. Each chapter is treated the same except for Chapter 7. The focus of Chapter 7 is skill development and growth opportunities rather than research. Because of this, the look, feel, and length of Chapter 7 is distinctive.

At the beginning of each chapter the first thing the reader will see is the Growing Teacher Leadership image. We think it is a good visual reminder and illustration of where the reader is in the seven-phase process.

After the Growing Teacher Leadership image is a segment where the authors take the opportunity to explain their understanding of and the importance of the "phase" in the development of teacher leadership.

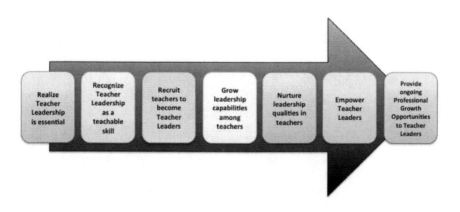

Figure 0.1.

PULSE CHECK

Quality administrators practice the art of self-reflection as a means to grow professionally. As you will read in Chapter 7, this practice is passed on in turn to active or aspiring teacher leaders they are currently working with. This portion of each chapter provides the reader a place to record their thoughts as they begin their journey through each chapter. Guiding questions will be provided in this section. Some of these questions will compel the reader to consider aspects of the phase that haven't yet been examined. This section also provides a means to make the findings in each phase relevant to their setting, experiences, and professional growth.

RESEARCH QUESTIONS AND EXPLANATION OF FINDINGS

In this section of each chapter, the questions that guided our research are disclosed. We began our journey toward understanding much like anyone else who has researched a particular topic. We had questions about teacher leadership that we thought needed to be answered. The findings would in turn inform our understanding of teacher leadership in general and a process to develop and grow teacher leadership in particular. Some sections contained three and others contained two research questions. The explanations of findings portion is just that, an explanation. We used as many excerpts from our research as we could in this section as well.

Anyone who has performed research can appreciate the emotions one goes through when analyzing the results. We have summarized these here and can attest to each one during this journey.

Pleased: We were pleased and content when our research affirmed that research that came before ours.

Excited: We felt excitement when our research offered what we believe was a new insight into the research and development of teacher leaders.

Confused: Anyone who has performed qualitative research understands this emotion. Countless hours were spent looking at some of the data that still has us questioning, "What exactly does this mean?"

Contemplative: We have researched and already written a book about teacher leadership. We both teach graduate-level courses about teacher leadership. It is hard, in our estimation, for any researcher not to have preconceived notions about the topic being examined. Some of what we discovered forced us to reconsider some of what we thought we knew about teacher leadership and offered an insight into future inquiry.

VIGNETTE

Quite possibly, the best way to gain an understanding of each phase is to read how others have dealt with each phase or how full implementation of the phase looks in other buildings. The vignettes offer practicing or aspiring teacher leaders an example of what to expect when the phase is fully completed. This section also allows the teacher leader to review and reflect on current practices and understanding of how the phase relates to their current process.

KEY TAKEAWAYS

This portion of each chapter is related to the Pulse Check segment studied previously. Key takeaways are components that we believe each administrator or aspiring teacher leader must understand to grow and develop teacher leaders in his or her building or district. Additionally, the section allows for readers to identify their own key takeaways from each phase. This is a way to reflect on your learning to grow teacher leadership or to develop as a teacher leader.

RECOMMENDATIONS

This portion of the chapter can be used as a checklist for the practicing administrator. Contained within this section are our recommendations for administrators who are using this book as a guide for growing teacher leaders. We also believe the concepts or ideas listed in this section characterize each phase. We gave special care to detailing some of the shortcomings of teacher leadership as it relates to the current phase. We feel it is imperative that what is recommended be completed or (in the works) before moving on to the next chapter.

CHAPTER SUMMARY

This section is at the end of each chapter and provides a clear, concise summary of everything found within the phase and indicators pertaining to the growth of teacher leadership.

ONE

Phase 1: Realize Teacher Leadership Is Essential

If you are reading this book, you have undoubtedly reached the conclusion that teacher leadership is needed or you are just beginning to explore teacher leadership for school improvement or transformation. In either situation, it is important to realize that teacher leadership is indeed essential in today's schools—no matter if it is a public, private, large, small, urban, or rural school. As a visual reminder, the figure below will be used throughout the book to show where we are in our examination of the process to grow and develop teacher leaders.

The process of realization is unique to all individuals, schools, and organizations. As a classroom teacher, did you realize you were not reaching and inspiring all of your students? As a coach, did you realize your athletes weren't performing to their highest potential? As a school

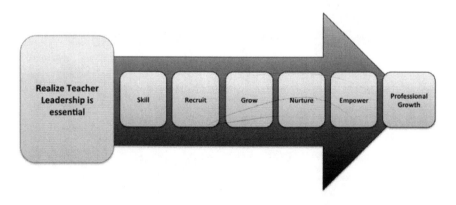

Figure 1.1.

administrator, when was it that you realized that the demands of your job were becoming so complex that you needed some type of support? The process or realization begins only after one reflects and contemplates on the results of a task or performance.

In the examples given, the classroom teacher, after realizing that not all of his students are learning the content, decides to differentiate his instruction and tier the lessons to meet the diverse needs of the students in his class. The coach decides to focus more on teamwork and encourages his players to be selfless and supportive teammates in both losing and winning efforts. The school administrator makes the decision to turn to those in her school that are best equipped to assist with the increasing complexities of education today, her teachers.

Teacher leadership is essential in today's schools. As schools continue to manage complex processes and issues like state and federal regulations, stagnant or decreasing school budgets, a more diverse student body, and an aging teacher workforce, the need for teacher leaders will only grow. The school administrator mentioned previously realized, after much thought and deliberation, that she needed to grow a culture of teacher leadership in her school. We further maintain that the culture of teacher leadership will lead to:

- *More collaboration among teachers.* When teachers collaborate and become a part of the decision-making process, they become more engaged in the school and committed to the school's vision.
- *A positive school culture.* Culture trumps strategy every day of the week. As a culture of teacher leadership grows, the school culture improves. In addition, it is important that culture determines the success of teacher leaders because the school's culture must be transformed from one of silos, top-down decisions, negativity to a culture of collaboration, shared decision making, positivity, and growth.
- *Teachers taking more risks and becoming more creative and innovative.* As teachers collaborate more, their confidence grows. They feel empowered to think outside the box because of the professional supports that collaboration provides.
- *Improved student achievement and professional practice.* Teacher leaders encourage others to share high-yield strategies that will lead to improved student achievement.
- *Empowerment of other stakeholders.* As teachers are empowered to be leaders, they, in turn, set a positive example for their colleagues to emulate.
- *Increased capacity for school transformation.* As teachers are empowered to be leaders, they can assist school administrators in transforming the school's culture. It is important to note, that school

transformation leads to school culture characterized by shared and collaborative leadership, which strengthens teacher leadership.

- *Improved school leadership.* As schools continue to increase in complexity, teacher leaders can help school administrators to be more effective instructional and operational leaders. School administrators can empower teacher leaders to take on more leadership roles such mentors, coaches, and facilitators, which will allow school administrators to have more time to be the school's instructional leader.

Before examining the research questions, we think it important for the practicing administrator to think about how teacher leadership will be communicated to your staff. Our recommendation is that it is never too early! Not everyone (including ourselves) understands the various nuances of the term *teacher leadership*. A part of our understanding, which has been mentioned previously, is derived from the Teacher Leader Model Standards.

An understanding of these standards provides foundational knowledge about what teacher leadership means to the Leadership Consortium members who drew them up. A more practical understanding of these standards is provided for those interested in our previous work, *The Leader Within.* We think it is incumbent for any administrator seriously thinking about growing teacher leadership to learn as much about the concept as they can.

Teacher leadership is unique in each school and district. Teacher leadership needs in school A is going to look and feel different in school B. The focus for school A might be community outreach, whereas in school B, the emphasis is on curriculum. Our contention is that the school administrator must not only consider how the needs of the school/district are communicated, but more importantly, how is teacher leadership (as defined by the needs of your school) communicated? In fact, celebrate and communicate the diversity of teacher leadership and the varying levels and processes of teacher leadership in schools. Differentiation of teacher leadership in each school is an advantage that must be recognized, celebrated, communicated, and embraced.

The communication of teacher leadership must be put in terms that are relevant to teachers and other stakeholders. School administrators must understand the preferences of their staff in terms of communication. In most cases, teachers prefer that school administrators are clear, concise, and transparent. It is essential that when recruiting teachers to be leaders, the school administrator clearly communicates the purpose of teacher leadership and the role the teacher leader will play in leading the school.

Communication as a strategy for recruiting teacher leaders must be strategically planned. Think about what your teachers need to hear that will encourage them to be leaders, as well as, support a culture of teacher leadership in the school. Communicating the overall goals and vision for teacher leadership must be a priority in designing your school's recruitment plan.

PULSE CHECK

Quality administrators practice the art of self-reflection as a means to grow professionally. This practice is passed on in turn to active or aspiring teacher leaders that they are currently working with. This portion of the book provides the reader a place to record their reflections as they make their way through each chapter—a way to show an understanding of the expectations for each phase—and provides a means to make the findings in each phase relevant to their setting, experiences, and professional growth.

The questions are designed to assist the administrator or teacher leader in their reflection. Use the space in between each question to record your answers.

- Have the efforts to grow a culture of teacher leadership in your school led to (a) More collaboration among teachers? (b) Teachers taking more risks and becoming more creative and innovative? (c) Improved student achievement? (d) Empowerment of all stakeholders?
- Has teacher leadership proven to be essential in your school's long-term success? If so, why? If not, why not?
- Are teacher leaders critical in your school's vision or long-term strategic plan, and if so, why?
- What events led to the administration's decision to grow a culture of teacher leadership?

In your school, do teacher leaders perform the following, and if so, how?

- Help colleagues work collaboratively
- Serve as team leaders
- Use knowledge of existing and emerging technologies (Internet, instructional applications, and social media) to promote collaborative learning
- Do teacher leaders have a positive impact on the rest of the staff and other stakeholders? If so, how?

EXPLANATION OF FINDINGS AND RESEARCH QUESTIONS

The three research questions that guided our research for the first phase were:

1. How are teacher leaders essential to your school's long-term success?
2. Why are teacher leaders critical in your school?
3. What was the epiphany when you realized the need for teacher leaders in your school?

The Difference Between Essential and Critical

On the surface level, essential and critical might seem to some to mean the same thing. In this context, teacher leaders being essential mean that they are necessary for the school's success in general. The term *critical* in this context means that teacher leaders are extremely important. Even the casual observer can see the difference between necessary and extremely important.

To acquire richer data in our first two questions we also asked how and why. For the first question, we were attempting to identify specific examples: duties and roles teacher leaders currently have in school districts. For the second question, we were trying to determine specific processes or activities that are currently being done or have been done in the past, by teacher leaders, which proved to be essential to the school or district.

The third research question genuinely gets to the heart of this phase of our research. "What was it that made you realize the importance of teacher leaders?" Obviously, the responses to this research question were indiscriminate and we knew they would be. There is no scientific process a person goes through when they come to realize something is important. What we were trying to establish were practical events or experiences that led one down the path to this realization.

During the "Realize" phase of growing teacher leaders, we identified three emerging themes from our research. These are Leadership Self-Fulfillment, Distributed Leadership, and Effects on Staff. It is important to remember that at this phase, the administrator or inquiring teacher leader has realized that teacher leadership is a necessity at his or her school or district. It should also be pointed out that many of the respondents used words associated with different phases like nurture, empower, and build.

As was explained previously in this chapter, the three research questions will no doubt elicit responses that described examples and activities teacher leaders have performed in the past. We look at this as a natural occurrence for those who know about and have fostered teacher leaders in the past. A list of the themes and an explanation of each is examined next. The portion of the text in quotes comes directly from our research.

Leadership Self-Fulfillment

Respondents at this stage seem to recognize that when they have empowered teachers to be leaders the result is that it strengthens the teacher's leadership ability. "Empowered teachers who feel confident to challenge the status quo by taking calculated risks are the lynchpin to fostering individual and systemic growth. They are the fuel that drives the engine." Many respondents explained how teacher leadership roles fulfilled an individual (leadership) need for some. "Teacher leadership provides growth opportunities which are motivating for those who wish to continue their career in the classroom or who wish to seek school leadership options." Additionally, "delegation to teacher leaders prepares the teachers to be future leaders."

It was obvious that those who participated in our research understood that teacher leaders are teachers, first and foremost. One respondent reported, "It provides a career path towards leadership without going into administration." A reoccurring theme in this phase was a focus on retention. Because teacher leadership fulfills a certain personal need, it "helps to retain good teachers and promote good teachers advancing within the profession." The quote that seems to summarize this section the best was "I saw the value of nurturing our teacher leaders in building a better sustainable leadership capacity at our school."

Furthermore, as subtly indicated by our research, school administrators increase their effectiveness as 21st-century organizational leaders when they empower teachers to be leaders. By creating collaborative leadership constructs and a culture of teacher leadership, school administrators can, instead of focusing on all aspects of the school, focus more on leadership, instead of management. School administrators often, as a result of the complexities that they face, resort to management skills to navigate the burdensome tasks associated with increasing bureaucracies.

Though paperwork will continue to be a cumbersome "thing to do," by empowering teachers to be leaders, instructional focus, student success, and professional growth will never take a back seat to low-priority tasks such as paperwork. As school administrators complete the daily to-do tasks, teacher leaders help keep the focus on the priority items such as effective teaching in the classroom, student advocacy, and new teacher supports—just to mention a few.

Distributed Leadership

We thought it was fitting that we begin this section with a quote from one of our practicing teacher leaders and her thoughts about distributed leadership following her internship.

> When I feel like my voice matters and that I play a role in building the school atmosphere, I am so much more willing to go the extra mile. I

want my students to care and be engaged, I need to involve them in decision-making, as I have been, and give them power in their education.

A 21st-century school is complex and requires a culture that is collaborative. "Teacher leaders are looked to by school administrators to be active in establishing a culture and, in many cases, are the change agents in the schools tasked with creating an environment conducive to collaboration" (Creasman & Coquyt, 2016, p. 3). Respondents for this phase suggested that the leadership (base) needed to be developed in their schools. "Continuous turnover is a natural and healthy part of a school's functioning. By broadening the leadership base, it ensures buy-in from teachers and the continuity of successful programs as positions change."

Another respondent asserts, "I realized quickly that I could not improve learning by myself. I needed to develop leadership in almost every grade level." Further evidence for the need for distributed leadership is embodied in the following statement, "Administrators can't do it alone. We must develop teacher leaders to help implement and support campus initiatives." According to Creasman and Coquyt (2016), "teacher leaders, in fact, often are looked to by both teachers and school administrators to be the leaders in leading processes that promotes an environment of collegiately, trust and mutual respect" (p. 3).

Just as the leader who opened this section stated that she saw herself as more than just a teacher, but a leader, many respondents answered in kind. "I realized that building the capacity of staff to see themselves as leaders and part of a team enabled greater learning and engagement across the schools." One administrator stated it aptly,

> Distributed leadership is the way to get improvement across the school, so I promote through an aspiring leaders group the opportunity to be involved in the decision making within the school and policy making. This enables all teachers to be involved, if interested, and spreads the load of responsibility across a number of staff.

In response to our question about the epiphany, a respondent reminded us,

> From our world's best workforce compliance, student handbook, staff handbook, curriculum creation, PLC's and Technology Initiatives we need our teachers to step up and help with the decision making process and running of the school. It wasn't a moment, it is a constant reality.

Effects on Staff

If there was one overarching theme running throughout this phase of our research it would be the effects teacher leaders, or potential teacher leaders, have on the colleagues they work with. In our book *The Leader Within* we used the *Nine Characteristics of High-Performing Schools*, developed by the Washington Department of Public Instruction, we attempt to differentiate between the work of educational leaders and that of teacher leaders (see Appendix B for the entire chart). In doing so, we have, in effect, identified many of the methods that teacher leaders use to affect or influence their colleagues. A few of these are:

- A teacher leader uses group processes to *help colleagues work collaboratively* to solve problems, make decisions, manage conflict, and promote meaningful change.
- A teacher leader *serves as a team leader to harness the skills, expertise, and knowledge of colleagues* to address curricular expectations and student learning needs.
- A teacher leader *uses knowledge of existing and emerging technologies to guide colleagues in helping students skillfully and appropriately navigate the universe of knowledge available on the Internet,* use social media to promote collaborative learning, and connect with people and resources around the globe.
- A teacher leader *uses opportunities not only to lead, but also to serve and empower others to be leaders.* Service, empowerment, and collaboration strengthens the culture of teacher leadership and also builds "bench depth" or leadership capacity in the school to transform.

One thing that we hypothesized before conducting our research was that the lens the respondents were looking through might elicit responses that would focus on how teacher leaders could assist the administration in various tasks and responsibilities. This was not the case at all. Most responses focused solely on how the teacher leaders influence those around them. "Teacher leaders are the change agents for our buildings. As leaders they participate in visioning our future. As a result, they help bring along the rest of the staff. Who better to lead than those most like you . . . your peers?"

Furthermore, "They are critical to fostering a culture of continuous improvement. Empowered teachers who feel confident to challenge the status quo by taking calculated risks are the lynchpin to fostering individual and systemic growth. They are the fuel that drives the engine." And finally, "Having observed various school communities for more than 21 years, the common thread of success in the class room is when teachers themselves become leaders and take personal responsibility for the success of their students as well as their peers."

A theme that came up time and time again in our research was how teacher leaders model best practices. For example,

> They model best practices, "infect" other teachers with the motivation to best adapt to school culture of excellence. Teacher leaders are generally happy in their respective positions and help fill the (break room) with an air of optimism looking forward; keeping all on trajectory of growth.

The term *best practices* is quite broad. Some of the respondents focused on best practices as they relate to classroom instruction. "Part of being a teacher leader is coaching and mentoring teachers. Modeling best practices within the classes, implementing teaching strategies and helping classroom teachers identify problems of practice and then to collect data to support if implemented strategies are working." We believe the following quote from our research sums up the variety of ways teacher leaders' influence their colleagues . . . as Gary Simms used to say, "You just can't make this stuff up."

To inspire and model best practice in teaching and learning; to mentor or coach others through various and differentiated collegial processes and practices; to help nurture a professional learning culture of collaboration and collegiality; to model ongoing learning and improvement for themselves and others; to foster and help grow problem-solving capacities of all staff; to share their own talents and expertise while facilitating for others to do the same; to take on high level and adaptable communications skills with all stakeholders, especially parents and caregivers; to grow productive and reciprocal networking opportunities beyond the school.

We couldn't have said it better ourselves.

VIGNETTE

Forest Ridge High School has been plagued with constant turnover of school administrators over the past 3 years. Each year, a new school administrative team is hired by the district, which results in low teacher morale, student achievement issues, and a bad school culture. As indicated by teachers and staff, it seems that with every new school administrative team, they are asked to do something new; they can never follow through on initiatives because they are asked to start new initiatives each year. Many of the teachers are now looking to leave the school at the end of the school year.

Facing low student achievement, a school culture that is disconnected, and a possible high turnover of teachers, the district hired Mrs. Weaver, a veteran school principal from a neighboring district and allowed her to hire two assistant principals of her choice. Before hiring the assistant principals, Mrs. Weaver met with the school leadership team made up of department chairs from each subject area (English, math, science, social studies, career-technical education, arts and humanities, and the counseling department).

By all accounts, the school's leadership team is strong and many parents, teachers, and district officials credit the leadership team for keeping the school functioning the past 3 years. As Mrs. Weaver met with the school leadership team, she quickly realized that the teachers wanted to have a voice in the school's direction, decision-making process, and leading the school. In the past, they had to operate behind the scenes because the previous school administrative team did not believe in a shared leadership structure and instead favored a centralized, top-down approach to leading the school.

Through her conversations with teachers and other stakeholders, Mrs. Weaver, realized, unlike in her previous experiences, that she had to actively engage teachers in the decision-making process. Fortunately for her, she had just returned from a workshop that dealt with creating a culture of teacher leadership in schools and how it led to school improvement and higher teacher morale. Using the information presented, Mrs. Weaver asked the district to pilot a teacher leadership program at her school for the upcoming school year. Instead of hiring two assistant principals, she would hire one assistant principal and one teacher leader.

She planned on using the teacher leader position to help her engage teachers in the decision-making process, establish a coaching and mentoring program, and begin to develop protocols for professional learning communities. Though this idea was somewhat controversial to the district, the local board of education, and many of the teachers at Forest Ridge High School, Mrs. Weaver was granted permission to pilot the teacher leadership program for the upcoming school year.

Working closely with the school's leadership team, she promoted a seasoned teacher at the school to teacher leader. Mrs. Weaver recognized that Sam Portersmith, a veteran science teacher at the school, was well respected by all members of the leadership team and had the motivation and personality that was needed to help the teacher leadership program to succeed and help engage teachers in the decision-making process, which would increase student achievement and staff morale and transform the school culture.

Though the idea of empowering a teacher to be a leader in the school, directly under the school principal in the organizational structure was seen by many as taboo in school leadership circles, Mrs. Weaver was comfortable with her own leadership style to share the leadership responsibilities and decision-making processes with a teacher. The results were almost instant, but the lasting result was far more rewarding for students, teachers, staff members, and other school stakeholders.

Forest Ridge High School, once seen as a failing school, quickly rose to be among the top schools, not only in the district, but also in the state. Furthermore, teacher leadership spread throughout the district as a result, which allowed more students and staff members to benefit from empowering teachers as leaders.

By realizing the need for teacher voice Mrs. Weaver empowered the school's new culture of teacher leadership. Though many viewed her move to elevate a teacher leader to a member of the school's leadership team as risky, it paid off. Over the next 3 years, Forest Ridge High School had remarkable growth in student achievement, the school's culture went from among the worst to among the best, and teacher turnover almost became non-existent overnight. As realized by Mrs. Weaver, teacher leadership can be a powerful transformative engine in schools.

PHASE 1 REALIZE RECOMMENDATIONS

This portion of the chapter can be used as a checklist for the practicing administrator. Contained within this section are our recommendations for administrators who are using this book as a guide for growing teacher leaders. We also believe the concepts or ideas listed characterize each phase. We feel it is imperative that the following be completed or (in the works) before moving on to the next chapter.

One of the topics covered is one that needs to be addressed as early as possible. In your quest to establish a school or district culture of acceptance and acknowledgement of the positive effects of teacher leadership, you must first practice some form of distributive leadership. At the very least, we feel it imperative that you have a building-level leadership team developed. This team should be made up of various grade-level representatives and a specialty group (community education, special education, parent–teacher organization) representative as well. If this isn't the case, the formation of such a group will mark the beginning of your attempts to change your school's systems and eventually the culture itself.

It isn't that easy, though. Putting a diverse group together and talking with them on a bi-weekly basis isn't going to cut it. Leithwood et al. (2006) posits, "distributed leadership, when not executed properly or when exclusively implemented in a 'top-down' approach, can be interpreted as misguided delegation or even coercion" (p. 55). Harris and Muijs (2002) more specifically state, "one of the main barriers to teacher leadership concern the 'top down' leadership model that still dominates in many schools" (pp. 3–4). Barth (2001) probably explains it best,

> It is risky for a principal to share leadership with teachers. Since principals will be held accountable for what others do, it is natural that they want evidence in advance that those they empower will get the job done well. Principals are also mindful of how much care, feeding, and handholding must go into helping the teacher leader. Given their own time crunches, many principals believe that it is more efficient to make decisions by themselves—to hire that new teacher rather than setting up, meeting with, and managing a committee to do so. (p. 444)

Fullan (2005) calms the waters by asserting, "Leadership (not leaders) is the key to the new revolution in education" (p. xi). It is never too early to begin practicing some form of distributive leadership at your school or district. Our recommendation is to start small and begin providing some platform where your teachers have a seat at the decision-making table.

Distributive Leadership

As you will soon read, schools that have established a distributive or collaborative leadership model have an easier time growing teacher leaders than those that don't. Simply put, teachers who are accustomed to being a part of the decision-making process will be easier to develop than those who are used to a top-down bureaucratic method where they have no, or very little, authentic decision-making authority.

Focus on Teacher Leaders

We recommend that you focus your efforts on those that want to remain in the classroom setting rather than on aspiring administrators. In our experience, administrators are short-timers in your district but teacher leaders stay. Boyd-Dimock and McGee (1995) argue that for most, the decision to take on leadership has been accompanied by a decision to get out of teaching and into administration. The leadership opportunities you provide for your teacher leaders may be just what they have been looking for to be gratified.

Begin Planting Teacher–Leadership Seeds

Obviously, you can't proclaim your support and confidence for the merits of teacher leadership one week and expect to have a roomful of recruits the next. The process of growing and developing teacher leaders takes time. Begin finding ways to cleverly plant the teacher leadership seeds. A couple of ideas might be to: (1) mention teacher leadership and provide a brief definition at the next schoolwide or districtwide meeting, (2) place an article about teacher leadership in your monthly faculty newsletter with an invitation for a follow-up meeting soon after publication; (3) post flyers or posters about teacher leadership opportunities throughout the school; (4) post information about teacher leadership on social media; and/or (5) have one-on-one conversations with teachers regarding teacher leadership opportunities within the school or district.

If you were able to check off these three Recommendations, then you are well on your way to developing teacher leaders in your school or district. If not, what steps can be made right now to address those unchecked?

KEY TAKEAWAYS

The key takeaways are components that we believe each administrator must understand to grow and develop teacher leaders in his or her building or district. Additionally, the section allows for readers to identify their own key takeaways from Phase 1. This is a way to reflect on your learning to grow teacher leadership or as a teacher leader.

- Realizing that growing and empowering teacher leaders in your building or district are unique and the events that lead to this realization will be different from school to school.
- Schools that use teacher leaders adhere to a type of distributive leadership model.
- Teacher leaders have a positive impact on their colleagues.
- Teacher leaders don't necessarily want to become administrators. Instead, their newfound leadership positions lead to a type of self-fulfillment that can't be realized in the classroom setting.
- Most administrators expect teacher leaders to model best practices in the areas of curriculum and instruction, mentoring, problem solving, and outreach to all stakeholders.
- School administrators must realize the importance of teacher leadership in their ability to be effective 21st-century school leaders.

List Your Own Takeaways in the Space Provided

_____

_____

_____

_____

CHAPTER SUMMARY

The realization that teacher leadership is essential in today's educational settings is the first phase in our seven-phase process of growing teacher leadership. The events or circumstances that lead to this realization are unique for each school, district, or individual. Our research has revealed three positive overarching themes that have come about for those individuals and schools who have embraced teacher leadership. These are:

1. *Leadership Self-Fulfillment* for those who have been placed in a teacher–leadership role. Bottom line, teachers searching for more

from the profession than they can get by being a classroom teacher decide to remain in education when they assume a leadership position in their school.

2. The establishment of a *Distributed Leadership model* provides an opportunity for stakeholders (not just administration) to have their voices heard. This model is closely tied to leadership self-fulfillment. Our research has shown that teacher leaders want and need to be a part of the decision-making process in their schools.

3. Schools that promote and use teacher leaders have found that these individuals have a *positive effect on their colleagues*. Many of the respondents stated that teacher leaders in their buildings model best practices that range from quality classroom instruction to a positive voice/attitude in the teacher's lounge.

Teacher leadership must be strategic, formal, as well as, informal and adaptable. Realizing teacher leadership is needed in schools must begin with the realization that schools are complex organizations and no matter how effective the school administrator is, his or her leadership is not sustainable as schools increase in complexity. It is incumbent on the school administrators, in partnership with teachers and other stakeholders, to take a careful look at teacher leadership as a means to create collaborative leadership constructs that will result in the leadership capacity that will truly lead to school transformation. School transformation is the result of partnerships, collaboration, and shared leadership.

TWO
Phase 2: Recognize Teacher Leadership as a Teachable Skill

At this point, readers may be asking themselves, "First we need to realize the importance of teacher leadership, now we need to recognize the skills? Where is the substance?" We will get to that. We think that it is important to seriously consider your understanding of teacher leadership before getting into the recruitment stage. This type of thinking is called *metacognition*, that is, thinking about one's thinking or the practices used to plan, monitor, and assess one's understanding and performance. Although not necessarily considered a characteristic or a skill a teacher leader should possess, metacognition was mentioned enough times in our research to be cited. In response to our skills-needed research question, one of our respondents asserted:

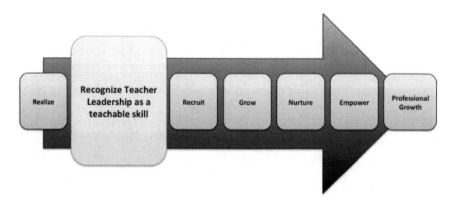

Figure 2.1.

15

Some of the skills teacher leaders need is knowledge of their strengths and weaknesses. Included is the ability to maintain composure under stressful situations and be effective communicators. They need knowledge of metacognition and willingness to be a reflective practitioner. Finally, they need the ability to establish and maintain interpersonal working relationships with people from all walks of life.

Researchers distinguish between metacognitive knowledge and metacognitive regulation (Flavell, 1979, 1987; Schraw & Dennison, 1994). Metacognitive knowledge refers to what individuals know about themselves as cognitive thinkers, about different approaches that can be used for learning and problem solving, and about the demands of a specific learning task. Metacognitive regulation refers to adjustments individuals make to their processes to help control their learning, such as planning, information-management strategies, comprehension monitoring, and evaluation of progress and goals. We contend that both metacognitive knowledge and regulation is important during the first two stages (and) something to keep in mind when working on developing your teacher leaders.

We assert that the skills that teacher leaders need are those proven to be highly effective, visible, and most importantly, teachable. Furthermore, as we have gathered through research and personal experience, the skills that teacher leaders possess are closely aligned to the school's vision and needs of stakeholders. For instance, one school may need teacher leaders who possess a variety of skills, and specifically communication skills. While on the other hand, another school may need teacher leaders who have experience and the skills to lead and facilitate professional learning communities.

By our estimation, the skills that teacher leaders need is very much a product of the school's culture and needs of the school's stakeholders. Additionally, one skill that is often overlooked in the research is the skill to adapt to any setting. Though mentioned below the surface in most research, we discovered that many administrators indicated that teacher leaders must have the ability to adapt to any situation and deploy skills that may not typically be used.

Leadership in and of itself might not be a teachable skill, but we contend that some of the skills associated with teacher leadership can be taught or learned. As you will read, our research during this phase studied skills and characteristics or dispositions. Our contention is that there are certain characteristics that most teacher leaders have, but some have skills that others do not. Our focus in Chapter 7 will be on leadership skills that can be taught or learned. We think it is important to differentiate between the two before moving forward.

PULSE CHECK

At this point, we recommend that school administrators begin to work closely with teachers and other stakeholders to determine the skills that are needed in your particular school. Do some potential teacher leaders possess these skills? Do they have certain characteristics that make them viable candidates for leadership positions?

It is incumbent on school administrators to evaluate the school's vision, current needs, and engage others in identifying the skills and characteristics teacher leaders will need to be successful in your school. What is true for one school or district may not be true for yours. Though many of the skills and characteristics that teacher leaders possess, like with other leaders, are universal, based on our research, we believe that teacher leaders must have specific characteristics and skills to be viable members of your leadership team.

Evaluate your school's leadership team by performing the activity that follows. Your answers can be written on the space provided in between each question.

- What are the current vital signs (mood and climate) of your school's leadership team? Are they trending in a positive direction or negative direction?

_____

_____

- What is the difference between a skill and a characteristic?

_____

_____

- What skillset do most of your current members bring to the table (and) can these skills be taught or learned?

_____

_____

- What characteristics do most of your current members possess?

_____

_____

- In your estimation, is your leadership team making progress?

_____

_____

- Are students succeeding as determined by preparedness for the next level?

_____

_____

Critical Skills: List the top five skills that you and your team consider most crucial in developing effective teacher leaders.

1. _____

2. _____

3. _____

4. _____

5. _____

Characteristics: List the top five characteristics that you and your team consider most crucial in developing effective teacher leaders.

1. _____

2. _____

3. _____

4. _____

5. _____

All of these are important to consider as school administrators work closely with teachers and other stakeholders when determining the characteristics and skillset needed by teacher leaders.

RESEARCH QUESTIONS AND EXPLANATION OF FINDINGS

The two questions that guided our research during this phase were:

1. What are the key characteristics or dispositions you look for in a prospective teacher leader?
2. What are the essential skills that teacher leaders must have to be effective leaders?

On further inquiry into these questions, readers might be asking themselves, "What is the difference between a characteristic and a skill?" For the purposes of our research, we thought it was important to differentiate between the two. A characteristic (also called a *quality* or *disposition*) is something that you would have been born with. It is something that will improve as you get older and gain more experience in teaching because it is a part of your personality. It is not something that you can learn to do; it is something that you just have. Our experience working with teachers have taught us that some are flexible, innovative, and modest. These are characteristics they were born with, not something that was acquired or learned.

A skill is something that you learn to do over a period of time. Through experience and training, you will learn new skills that can be used for different things. For example, in our experience, one skill that most first-year teachers struggle with is classroom management. Reading literature about the topic, talking with veteran teachers, and acquiring training will no doubt help develop classroom management skills. There is no substitute for experience, though. Experience allows you to hone your skills; taking bits and pieces from what you have learned and determining what will work for you.

When we were preparing for our research there were two undeniable truths about this phase that we discussed at length. First, there has been a lot of research done before ours about teacher leadership characteristics or dispositions. We believe identifying those who possess certain leadership characteristics is a crucial step to be done before the third phase, recruitment. If the teachers don't possess the necessary characteristics, they might not be worth your time and effort. Second, our research is, and has been tied closely to the Teacher Leader Model Standards (TLMS). In *The Leader Within*, we analyzed and dissected each domain and function meticulously.

The standards themselves contain numerous teachable or learnable skills that all practicing teacher leaders must possess. Much like characteristics, there will, no doubt, be teachers that already possess certain leadership skills that you may want to recruit to be a part of your leadership team. Anything that we could garner above and beyond what was already determined in previous research or what was mentioned in the standards regarding characteristics and skills would be considered a bonus.

As mentioned, many research articles have been published about the characteristics or dispositions that teacher leaders must possess. A short list is provided in the table that follows.

Author, Date	Characteristic(s)
Collins, 2001	Humility
Kouzes and Posner, 2002	Credibility
Badarocco, 2002	Modesty
Allio, 2005	Character
	Creativity
	Compassion
York-Barr & Duke, 2004	Collaborative
	Dependable
	Supportive
	Knowledgeable
·	Flexible
Crowther, Kaagan, Ferguson, & Hann, 2009	Professional Image
	Trustworthy
Rosenholtz, 1989	Hard Worker
Wilson, 1993	Innovative
	Motivational
	Dedicated
Strodl, 1992	Reassuring to Colleagues

Our research attempted to see if any other characteristic or disposition made the list. We hypothesize that the dispositions needed in 2017 might be different from those in 2005 because of the ever-evolving nature of education.

Jonathan Doh's (2003) work on leadership is, in our estimation, one of the best articles written on the topic of whether leadership skills can be taught. As he so aptly stated, "as educators, we should be skeptical of our ability to mold leaders, and instead should view leadership as one of several characteristics and skill sets that may be further developed by education and practice" (p. 66). Allio (2005) contends, "While leadership cannot be taught, leadership can be learned" (p. 1071). He goes on to state, "most leadership training initiatives teach theory, concepts, and principles; they promote leadership literacy but not leadership competence." (p. 1071).

In the article, Allio's statements about selecting the right candidates (Phase 3), creating learning challenges (Phases 4–5), and providing mentoring (Phase 6) were instrumental in the development of our seven-phase plan for growing teacher leaders. As you will read in Chapter 7, our focus will be on teacher leader skills that can be taught or leaned.

Research Question: What are the key characteristics (or dispositions) you look for in a prospective teacher leader?

The characteristics that quality teacher leaders do or should possess are many and wide-ranging. The table provides the reader with a short list of some of the most prevalent characteristics determined by previous research. Our research produced nine predominant characteristics that current administrators thought important for teacher leaders to possess. These are:

1. *Outside the box thinking; innovative*
2. *Risk-taker*
3. *Growth mind-set*
4. **Passionate**
5. *Empathetic*
6. *Respected or respect for colleagues*
7. *Good communicator/listener*
8. *Quality teaching*
9. **Initiative**

The characteristics that are *italicized* are those that have been thoroughly investigated in previous research. Rosenholtz's (1989) and Wilson's (1993) research put forward that teacher leaders are innovative risk-takers who inspired their colleagues to be problem solvers. The idea of teacher leaders as (risk-takers) and quality teaching was mentioned in York-Barr and Duke's (2004) research.

Crowther, Kaagan, Ferguson, and Hann (2002) conducted a 5-year study of schools in Australia. This research identified characteristics regarding respect, growth mind-set, and translating ideas into actions. Regarding empathy, Allio (2005) argues, "No leadership program even attempts to engender compassion on the part of its students, to infuse them with emotional intelligence, a concept that has been actively promoted in recent leadership initiatives" (p. 1073).

What our research on teacher leader characteristics might add to this conversation are passion and initiative. Communication also made our list, but we believe this belongs in the skills section. A caveat about our research and what we have learned along the way is in order before proceeding. In our research, and in research done about teacher leadership, we have found that the terms *characteristics* and *skills* have sometimes been used interchangeably.

Our contention is that potential leaders possess many characteristics that they bring to the table without formal training. They are born with it and it is a part of their personality. This entire book is devoted to growing and developing teacher leaders. Our focus will be on skills that can be learned (through experience) or taught. As you will soon read, many teacher leadership skills are different from the skills administrators must have. Some may already possess some of these skills, which is always a benefit to administrators.

Passion

Passion, or being passionate about teaching, is something that is absent from teacher leadership literature. Our experiences as administrators have provided us with numerous examples of teachers who were passionate about what they do in their classrooms each day. It is a pleasure and a joy to be in their classrooms; to see how their students fed off their passion. Passionate teachers require them to be open to change. Passionate teachers reflect on their practice and experiment with ways to become more effective in the classroom.

This is done in a variety of ways like integrating technology, adapting practices to address the needs of diverse learners, understanding different learning styles, and providing students choices. Passionate teachers create an active, collaborative learning environment where students discover knowledge. We really don't think that anyone can argue that passion can be taught. You either have it, or you don't. In our experience, this passion often times spills over and affects the entire school community.

Teacher leaders are passionate about ensuring student success through service, collaboration, and leadership. As we mentioned in *The Leader Within*, teacher leadership, at the end of the day, is always about student success. Teacher leaders have a laser focus on implementing processes that will lead to student success and creating the best learning programs that will lead to student engagement. Their passion continues outside the classroom by ensuring that they mentor and coach teachers and facilitate professional learning opportunities for professional growth. Furthermore, they are passionate about creating a culture of collaboration and shared decision making. Teacher leaders view collaborative leadership constructs as an engine that will transform the school and culture.

Initiative

In our experience working with, teaching in higher education, and with our research in teacher leadership, the term *initiative* has been discussed quite often. As the long list of teacher leader characteristics mentioned previously suggests, most teacher leaders are not satisfied with the status quo. A frustration that many teacher leaders face is the bureaucracy of education. Teacher leaders don't passively wait for their principal or upper administration to inform them how to address such things as 21st-century college- and career-readiness standards.

Instead, they take the initiative to research the subject and put forth a plan detailing how they will address the standard in their teaching. Teacher leaders don't always adhere to the rigid pacing guides that hamstring them from using supplemental materials they know will enhance their teaching and their students' learning. One respondent stated, "Teacher leaders are actively searching for new information to help support what they do and what our school needs."

Because of the nature of our research methodology, specific actions or initiatives taken by teacher leaders were not included in this part of our research. We sought out examples of teacher leader characteristics, not necessarily specific examples. In *The Leader Within*, we present numerous explicit examples of teachers leaders that have taken the initiative to address issues in their school or district that are related to the TLMS (Appendix B). An example from Domain 7 follows.

The teacher leader uses a variety of techniques to share relevant local, state, and national trend information with their colleagues. Together, the principal and teacher leader discuss opportunities and how to disseminate this information. Some of the more common examples are e-mail, staff meetings, newsletters, and a "flipped" communication method.

Some teacher leaders have decided to differentiate their communication methods and offer their teachers a "flipped" trends and policy lesson each month. These teacher leaders videotape themselves, providing a summary of the most recent local, state, and national trends and policies, and share the link with their colleagues. Teachers can view the link at their leisure. If they have questions or concerns, they can meet with the teacher leader at a predetermined location one week after the link was sent.

As indicated, just as specific examples of characteristics were not asked for during this phase of our research, the same is true for skills. We were seeking out the skill itself rather than examples of the skill. It bears repeating that certain teachers that you will recruit (Phase 3) will already possess certain characteristics and skills before they take on the role of a teacher leader. There isn't much you can do about the characteristics, but skills, and specific teacher leadership skills, can be learned or taught.

Research Question: What are the essential skills that teacher leaders must have to be effective leaders?

One of the more interesting things we discovered during this portion of our research was that many of the respondents used the terms *skills* and *characteristics* interchangeably. For instance, communication, in our estimation, is a skill that can be learned. Many respondents also listed communication skills as a characteristic. The same is true for quality teaching, listed as both a characteristic and a skill. This is one of many things that we wish we would have done better in our research. We should have differentiated between a skill and a characteristic before the respondents completed the survey questions.

The other curious aspect during this phase of our research was the absence of many of the teacher leader skills listed in the TLMS. Last, we found it refreshing that our respondents, in keeping with true qualitative research design, not only listed the skill, but in many cases also provided an explanation that allowed a deeper analysis of the responses, which in turn generated richer data.

The skills that quality teacher leaders do or should possess are as diverse as the characteristics. As mentioned previously, our work is tied closely to the TLMS. A detailed analysis of the skills teacher leaders need is clearly stated within the standards. Our analysis of teacher leader skills will be as follows:

1. List of the top five skills from our research.
2. Briefly discuss those skills in the TLMS that are absent from our research.

Top Five Skills

Quality Teaching/Instruction

Quality teaching and effective instructional practices were mentioned numerous times by our respondents in both the characteristics and skills portion of our research. We believe it belongs in the skills portion simply because the skills needed to become a quality teacher are learned through experience and training. Furthermore, these skills can be taught and learned. One may have the dispositions necessary to become a quality teacher, but without the needed skills they will never reach their fullest potential. One of our respondents suggested that teacher leaders "lead on the campus while still maintaining excellence in their own classroom." Many respondents simply reported "strong teaching or quality teaching" without going into specifics. Although difficult to quantify, some of what constitutes quality teaching or quality instruction involves:

- A teacher leader facilitates the collection, analysis, and use of classroom—and school-based data to identify opportunities to improve curriculum, instruction, assessment, school organization, and school culture (TLMS Domain 4 Function A).
- A teacher leader uses knowledge of existing and emerging technologies to guide colleagues in helping students skillfully and appropriately navigate the universe of knowledge available on the Internet, uses social media to promote collaborative learning, and connects with people and resources around the globe (TLMS Domain 4 Function E).
- A teacher leader facilitates the analysis of student learning data, collaborative interpretation of results, and application of findings to improve teaching and learning (TLMS Domain 2 Function B).

Communication

In many cases, teacher leaders perform communication differently as they seek to use communication to engage diverse perspectives in the decision-making process. Teacher leaders understand that communication is the mechanism that engages and empower others. Teacher leaders often use one-on-one mentoring as the medium of choice to communicate to teachers, teacher leaders, and other stakeholders. Though teacher leaders use all available tools (such as: social media and e-mail) to communicate, they overwhelmingly prefer the face-to-face communication. They understand how relationships impact communication.

It takes years of practice to become a good communicator. Teacher leaders, much like administrators, need to develop exceptional communication skills as well as other skills that also make the list. As one of our respondents so aptly stated:

> Given that CHANGE is impacting hugely on education at the moment (and much of it appropriate), the ability to enact change is crucial together with all the other attributes that contribute to that ability. A good communicator (includes listening), great interpersonal skills, the ability to create cohesion and common purpose in a team.

Strodl (1992) indicated that teacher leaders have excellent communication skills as compared to their colleagues. Finally, one of our respondents linked communication with a very important disposition, dependability:

> Communication skills and dependability are very important. Not what is communicated, but how it's communicated is very important. And, being dependable . . . when you can count on someone to handle things and not have to go back and re-do or make sure it was communicated effectively . . . very important.

Listening and Relationships (Collaboration)

Respondents listed listening as a skill teacher leaders must possess. Robert Greenleaf (1998) posits, "the inability to listen may be the most costly of the human relations skills to be without" (p. 71). We have decided to combine these two skills because they are so closely related. As in *The Leader Within*, we turn to Jim Knight for his expertise and advice on the topics of listening and relationships. Regarding authentic listening, Knight states, "We struggle to listen simply because we may not want to hear what others are saying" (p. 61). He goes on to assert, "We are usually drawn to those messages that confirm our hopes or affirm our assumptions about ourselves" (p. 61). We will revisit listening as a skill and examine particular strategies teacher leaders can practice and learn in Chapter 7.

Building relationships and the ability to collaborate were two skills our respondents mentioned quite frequently. Here, a respondent explains their thoughts about which skills are imperative for teacher leaders.

> The combination of understanding ones' own core beliefs and the ability harness the energy and thoughts of all stakeholders in the vision of the school/district. They must have the skills to listen for understanding, be an effective communicator, and be able to collaboratively work with others.

Jim Knight's (2007) *Instructional Coaching*, specifically Chapter 3, focuses on what Knight calls the partnership philosophy. Functioning as an instructional coach is one of many roles a teacher leader may perform in a school system. According to the partnership philosophy, instructional coaches "see themselves as equal, respect others' choices, and encourage others to voice opinions" (p. 40). The partnership philosophy is designed to build a trusting relationship between the instructional coach and the teacher with whom they are working. We will reexamine building relationships as a skill and examine certain strategies teacher leaders can practice and learn in Chapter 7.

Big Picture

Many respondents mentioned big picture as a skill that teacher leaders must possess to be an effective leader. Teacher leaders see the big picture by staying out of the weeds (those areas that are designed to distract leaders from the purpose and vision of the school). Furthermore, they understand that at the end of the day, no matter what, teacher leaders are focused on the success of students and ensuring systems are in place that will lead to the students experiencing success. This requires that teacher leaders develop and lead professional learning communities, design protocols for coaching and mentoring teachers, and focus on the overall culture of the school. To remain focused on the big picture teacher leaders do not involve themselves in the redundancies of day-to-day operations because they are not micromanagers. In fact, they are visionary, transformative school leaders whose sole purpose is to help others remain focused on the big picture . . . the teaching and learning process.

The advantage of school administrators empowering teachers to be leaders is the mere fact, that they have another leader who is also focused on the big picture. As the complexities in schools continue to increase, school administrators and the overall school cannot afford not to focus on the big picture of educating students.

We assert that it is difficult to determine exactly what the big picture means and what it means might be different for each school or district. One respondent stated:

I believe they need to be able to see the big picture. They need to be able to see down the road and know how to go back to go forward. They need to understand that everyone has a perspective and for that person it is their reality. They need to understand how to lead people as well as when to consult with them. There is a difference.

Big-picture thinking was often associated with the word *vision*. One administrator responded, "The combination of understanding ones' own core beliefs and the ability to harness the energy and thoughts of all stakeholders is the vision of the school/district."

Organization

Organization, like big picture, is a term that came up repeatedly in our survey. Most of our respondents mentioned something about time management. One of our respondents stated, "My teacher leaders maintain organization through being good planners, setting goals for themselves, and, believe it or not, their classrooms and workspaces are always clean."

TLMS and Skills

As we stated previously, much of our previous research was done using the TLMS as a conceptual framework. Careful examination of the standards elicits certain skills that all teacher leaders must either possess or should be taught. Those skills that were mentioned in our current research and are also a part of the skills cited in the TLMS are quality teaching, listening, collaboration, and communication. We would be remiss if we didn't also examine the skills mentioned in the TLMS.

The following section features skills identified in the standards and a brief examination of each. A more thorough examination of each skill can be found in *The Leader Within*. We will also be revisiting these skills in Chapter 7. The Domain or Function from the TLMS where the skill is most prevalent is listed at the beginning of the description. It should be noted that the Domain and Function cited is used as one of the many examples that exist in the standards for teacher leaders.

Facilitation

TLMS Domain 4: Facilitating Improvements in Instruction and Student Learning. A facilitator is a guide to help people move through a process together, not the seat of wisdom and knowledge. This means that a facilitator isn't there to give opinions, but to draw out opinions and ideas of the group members. Facilitation focuses on how people participate in the process of learning or planning, not just on what gets achieved. A teacher leader often acts as a facilitator when working with colleagues. This skill is necessary to keep all group members engaged and ensure a positive outcome.

Advocacy/Presenting Ideas

Domain 7: Advocating for Student Learning and the Profession. Advocating for education is an essential skill that all teacher leaders must possess. Cuthbertson (2014) states, "Seeing ourselves as teacher-leaders and advocates for public education is key. If we don't see ourselves in this role, we leave the door open for others outside the profession to tell our stories and determine the successes (and shortcomings) of our schools." It can be as simple as a one-on-one conversation with a parent or as detailed as preparing public comments and testifying before a local school board, state board of education, or other governing body.

Modeling

Domain 1 Function B: The teacher leader models effective skills in listening, presenting ideas, leading discussions, clarifying, mediating, and identifying the needs of self and others in order to advance shared goals and professional learning. Modeling describes the process of learning or acquiring new information, skills, or behavior through observation, rather than through direct experience or trial-and-error efforts. Learning is viewed as a function of observation, rather than direct experience (Holland & Kobasigawa, 1980). Modeling, as it is related to teacher leadership, is most often related to classroom instructional practices.

Research

Domain 2: Accessing and Using Research to Improve Practice and Student Learning. In our experience, the most-common type of research that is performed in the K–12 setting is action research. Ash and Persall (2000) define action research as the "implementation of innovative practices coupled with an assessment of those practices on student learning" (p. 18). Richard Sagor (2000) asserts,

> Practitioners who engage in action research inevitably find it to be an empowering experience. Action research has this positive effect for many reasons. Obviously, the most important is that action research is always relevant to the participants. Relevance is guaranteed because the focus of each research project is determined by the researchers, who are also the primary consumers of the findings. (p. 1)

Reflective Practices

Domain 4 Function B: The teacher leader engages in reflective dialog with colleagues based on observation of instruction, student work, and assessment data and helps make connections to research-based effective practices. Teacher leaders practice the art of self-reflection as a means to grow professionally. They also understand that the most important choices teachers will make is how to make sense of whatever it is that they are learning with their colleagues. Knight (2007) contends, "Reflective thinkers, by definition, have to be free to choose or reject ideas, or else they simply are not thinkers at all" (p. 47).

According to Schon (1987), reflection is necessary for learning since often the most important parts of skillful or artistic activities, like teaching, are hidden from our conscious understanding. He goes on to insist, "People are skilled or artistic practitioners because they have a repertoire of competencies and skills that they may not even be able to identify" (p. 48).

Adult Learning Theory

A working knowledge of Adult Learning Theory is needed for teacher leaders because, after all, working with adults is much different than working with children. Andragogy (adult learning) is a theory that holds a set of assumptions about how adults learn. It uses approaches to learning that are problem based and collaborative rather than didactic (traditional lecturing or teacher "knows all" model), and also recognizes more equality between the teacher and learner.

A comprehensive understanding of adult learning principles is crucial to developing successful education programs that result in participant engagement and the facilitation of learning. Adults have special needs and requirements as learners. This skill is vital for teacher leaders to perform their job effectively.

VIGNETTE

Dr. Lynn is a 20-year veteran principal of the Bridgeport Academy, one of the first Montessori school in the Pilgrim Landing School District. Dr. Lynn is known for helping teacher leaders to grow the skills necessary to be effective. He understands how to evaluate teachers for strengths and growth opportunities and then aligns experiences that will help teacher leaders to develop their current skills while they acquire new skills.

As mentioned, Bridgeport Academy is a Montessori School, which provides school administrators and teachers more freedom to explore new innovative instructional strategies. But through innovation, Dr. Lynn uses the school's innovative culture to also grow teacher leaders. His trick is that he truly evaluates potential teacher leaders. He evaluates the prospective teacher leaders against the needs of the school, the students, the teachers, and the school administration. He is considered a guru when it comes to spotting "diamonds in the rough" and knows how to recruit and bring the best out of potential teacher leaders.

Once he evaluates the teacher leader(s), Dr. Lynn develops a personalized leadership plan for each one. The evaluation of the prospective teacher leader prioritizes the skills that are needed—aligned to the leadership areas of communication, transformation, service, innovation, and student success. The personalized leadership plan, according to Dr. Lynn, has truly been the game changer for growing and developing teacher leaders: The most veteran teacher leaders at Bridgeport Academy are still using the personalized leadership plan to continually improve and grow.

Instead of focusing on several skills to grow or improve, teacher leaders are assigned specific skills to focus on per academic year. Instead of trying to "boil the ocean" by focusing on several skills per year, Dr. Lynn believes that by focusing on one to two skills per year, teacher leaders can fine-tune their leadership, focusing on actually leading and not checking boxes and meeting benchmarks.

Dr. Lynn's technique is more about developing and acquiring the skills—not with timetables but with a clear focus on student achievement, school improvement, and leadership development. He prefers to strategically develop the skills, instead of focusing on a cookie-cutter approach, taking the time to develop the skills uniquely aligned to the individual teacher leader and the needs of the school.

PHASE 2 RECOGNIZE RECOMMENDATIONS

Similar to Chapter 1, this portion of the chapter can be used as a checklist for the practicing administrator. Contained within this section are our recommendations for administrators who are using this book as a guide for growing teacher leaders. We also believe the concepts or ideas listed characterize or distinguish each phase. We feel it is imperative that the following be completed or (in the works) before moving on to the next chapter.

Prior to examining our recommendations we thought it would benefit the reader to consider a few teacher leader skill-related items. Take into account the fact that the majority of your teachers are skilled at teaching children, adolescents, or young adults. Moller and Pankaka (2013) warn that they may lack the skill to coach or instruct other teachers. Barth (2001) speaks directly to this concern by affirming, "Many school faculties are congenial, but few would characterize themselves as collegial. Many teachers seem to lack the personal, interpersonal, and group skills essential to the successful exercise of leadership" (p. 82).

Our recommendation is to reflect on how often your teachers instruct each other and how mutually respectful your teachers have been toward one another in the past. If there has been opposition in the past, this may hinder your efforts to establish a culture of teacher leadership in your school.

Teacher Leader Characteristics and Skills

During this phase, it is imperative that the administrator have a good understanding of the prominent characteristics and skills most teacher leaders possess. This chapter contains many of the most-common teacher leader characteristics. Our recommendation is that you put yourself in a position to see or witness these characteristics first hand. We argue that the skills teacher leaders need most can be taught. The only skill that matters at this point is leadership, something most administrators know a thing or two about. Teaching specific teacher leader skills will be covered in Chapter 7.

Advance Your Teacher Leader Knowledge Base

Teacher leadership is not a new concept, but it may be new to your teachers and some of your administrative colleagues. There are plenty of quality articles you can research that will further your understanding of teacher leadership. Here is the link to the TLMS (http://www.gtlcenter.org/sites/default/files/docs/TeacherLeaderModelStandards.pdf), which is where we found most of the information and evidence for *The Leader Within*; this text would be an excellent resource for you and your colleagues to broaden your knowledge about teacher leadership.

If you were able to check off these two Recommendations, you are well on your way to beginning the process of recruiting those that you believe have the dispositions and skills necessary to become a member of your leadership team. If not, what steps can be made right now to address those unchecked?

KEY TAKEAWAYS

The key takeaways are components that each administrator or aspiring teacher leader must understand to grow and develop teacher leaders in his or her building or district. Additionally, the section allows for readers to identify their own key takeaways from Phase 2. This is a way to reflect on your learning to grow teacher leadership or to develop as a teacher leader.

- Recognize the characteristics and skills that are necessary for teacher leader growth and development.
- Recognize the difference between teacher leader characteristics and skills. As an administrator, you are in a better position if some of your teachers have the characteristics and not the skills. We contend that teacher leadership skills can be taught. It is more difficult

to develop a potential teacher leader who doesn't possess the necessary characteristics to lead.

- Leadership, specifically, the skills that accompany leadership, can be learned or taught.
- The TLMS contain many examples of characteristics and skills that teacher leaders need to possess.
- Skills in teaching, listening, collaboration, and communication are vital for teacher leaders to possess or acquire.
- School administrators must recognize the importance of teacher leadership in their ability to be effective 21st-century school leaders.

List Your Own Takeaways in the Space Provided

_____

_____

_____

_____

CHAPTER SUMMARY

The recognition of particular characteristics and skills essential to the development of teacher leadership is the second phase in our seven-phase process of growing teacher leadership. Where the characteristics or dispositions teacher leaders possess are somewhat universal, the skills needed by teacher leaders are unique for each school, district, or individual. We content that potential teacher leaders must possess certain characteristics or dispositions that many previous researchers have already identified.

These characteristics coupled with specific teachable skills are essential to growing teacher leaders. Our research has revealed two positive teacher leader characteristics that have come about for those individuals and schools who have embraced teacher leadership. These are:

1. *Passion.* Passionate teacher leaders reflect on their practice and experiment with ways to become more effective in the classroom. This is done in a variety of ways like integrating technology, adapting practices to address the needs of diverse learners, understanding different learning styles, and providing students choices. Passionate teachers create an active, collaborative learning environment where students discover knowledge.

2. *Initiative.* Teacher leaders take the initiative to research and address issues in their school or district without begin told. As previously stated, teacher leaders are actively searching for new information to help support what they do and what their schools need.

The art of leadership, be it organizational leadership, educational leadership, instructional leadership, or teacher leadership is based on particular skills. It is important to understand that the skills teacher leaders need to have to be effective are determined by the needs found in the school. Though certain skills may not be developed or acquired, nevertheless, school administrators must assist teacher leaders in developing the skills.

Here again, the success of teacher leaders is determined directly by the involvement and support of the school administration. The size or scope of the skill development should not deter school administrators or the teacher leader. The actual development of the skill—the journey to growing the bench of school leaders—must be embraced and welcomed.

Our research has revealed many teacher leader skills that have come about for those individuals and schools who have embraced teacher leadership. These are:

1. Quality Teaching
2. Communication
3. Listening/Collaboration
4. Big Picture
5. Organization

We contend that additional skills addressed in the TLMS should be added to the list. These include:

1. Facilitation
2. Advocacy/Presenting Ideas
3. Modeling
4. Research
5. Reflection
6. Adult Learning Theory

As teacher leaders develop or acquire the skill(s) necessary to be effective in their school, the overall culture of the school improves, as does student achievement. Skill development, if you will, is the opportunity to push the boundaries that typically hinder school improvement and leadership development.

THREE

Phase 3: Recruit Teacher Leaders

At this stage in our process, you are ready to begin recruiting those individuals that you deem worthy of either becoming a part of your leadership team or have the potential to be quality teacher leaders. The realization that teacher leadership is essential naturally led to a thoughtful assessment of who, in your teaching ranks, possess the characteristics and possibly already have the skills necessary to become a teacher leader. We have found in our research that there isn't one universal method or approach administrators use to recruit. The one constant is that the recruitment of teachers to be leaders must be strategic and planned.

The school administrator must not forget, as discussed in Chapter 2, that the recruitment of teachers must be aligned to the skills needed in the school. The school administrator must recruit teachers to become leaders who possess or can acquire the skills necessary to not only be

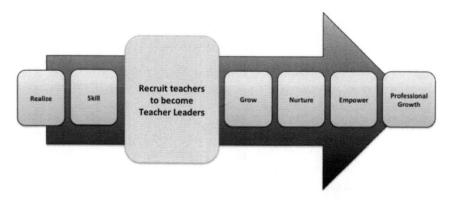

Figure 3.1.

effective, but will also fill a gap in the school. So when we talk about being strategic, skill recruitment is crucial in the recruitment of teacher leaders.

One respondent's recruitment style, whose method we do not recommend, stated bluntly, "church style, just go up to them and ask." The school administrator must use the techniques that he or she is most comfortable with throughout the recruitment process. More importantly, the administrator must use techniques and strategies that are effective and results in the best teachers being recruited into leadership positions. Teacher leadership is very important, therefore, the recruitment process must not be taken lightly and delegated.

A hypothetical human resources recruitment plan that many of you have probably used in your hiring process follows.

Step 1: Identify Vacancy and Evaluate Need
Step 2: Develop Position Description
Step 3: Develop Recruitment Plan
Step 4: Select Search Committee
Step 5: Post Position and Implement Recruitment Plan
Step 6: Review Applicants and Develop Short List
Step 7: Conduct Interviews
Step 8: Select Hire
Step 9: Finalize Recruitment

Our recruitment plan is a little less formal and a bit more individual or personal. At the third phase—recruitment—the administrator is already at Step 8 according to the hypothetical. At this phase, the administrator has certain individuals in mind that have the characteristics and skills necessary to be teacher leaders in their district.

School administrators and teachers who are thinking about implementing a culture of teacher leadership must understand the importance of culture in the overall recruitment process. Just like in other organizations, "culture trumps strategy" every day of the week. To encourage others to support a culture of teacher leadership, school administrators must clearly communicate the advantages of teacher leadership in schools. For instance, school administrators must take the time to research teacher leadership, and we strongly recommend visiting schools that have a culture of teacher leadership already established.

Additionally, as school administrators visit other schools, we strongly recommend taking teachers to also visit the schools. Teachers, as well as other stakeholders, need to see teacher leadership in action. Here again, if the school administrator is transparent about teacher leadership, by inviting others to help investigate teacher leadership, that will help to support teacher leadership in their school.

PULSE CHECK

As stated previously, this portion of the book provides the reader a place to record their reflections as they make their way through each chapter — a way to show an understanding of the expectations for each phase. This section provides a means to make the findings in each phase relevant to their setting, experiences, and professional growth. Use the spaces between each question to record your thoughts.

- List examples of when you have explained or discussed the importance of teacher leadership to a group (or) an individual staff member. If you haven't, are there future opportunities where this might be appropriate?

_____

_____

- In your district, how are teachers encouraged to seek out leadership opportunities?

_____

_____

- How comfortable are you discussing the topic of teacher leadership? If you are a bit apprehensive, where can you go to find more information about teacher leadership?

_____

_____

- How are the needs of your school or district communicated to your teachers?

_____

_____

- Think about an instance when you needed to encourage or inspire a staff member or group to do or try something new. Were you successful? Could a similar plan be used to encourage teachers in your building to seek leadership positions?

_____

_____

Research Questions and Explanation of Findings

The three questions that guided our research during this phase were:

1. How is the importance of teacher leadership communicated to stakeholders?
2. How are teachers encouraged to become teacher leaders?
3. What are the major components of your recruitment plan for teacher leaders?

One of the many things that motivated us to write *The Leader Within* was that we came to realize the importance of using teacher leaders not only in our professional lives as administrators, but as college instructors as well. Professionally, we were able to experience the benefits of employing a distributive leadership model and work with and eventually empowering many remarkable teacher leaders. As instructors in higher education, we were given the opportunity to research and teach many graduate-level courses that focused on teacher leadership. The combination of our experience and research brought us to a point where we could write intelligently about the subject of teacher leadership in a pragmatic manner.

Teacher leadership is not a new concept. As we wrote in *The Leader Within*, "Teacher leaders have been in our schools for decades, always leading from behind, connecting the dots for others, mentoring, coaching, and advocating for teachers and the profession" (p. x). Just because teacher leadership isn't new doesn't mean that every district uses it in some way, shape or form. Katzenmeyer and Moller (2001) argue, "Confusion and expectations of teacher leaders abound" (p. 4–5).

Wynne (2001) suggests that teacher leadership differs from the traditional bureaucratic method of leadership by the focus on teamwork. Many authors that have come before us have written about why teacher leaders are important in today's schools (DuFour & Eaker, 1998; Barth, 1991; Crowther, Kaagan, Ferguson & Hann, 2002; Donaldson, 2006). Ackerman and Mackenzie (2006) posit that teacher leaders can bridge the disparity between the ideal school setting and the current reality in education.

As stated previously in the Preface, a part of our research methodology was to seek out administrators who used teacher leaders or had experience working with teacher leaders. A careful examination of our research questions bears witness to this. We sought to find out answers to two important components to the recruitment process: how is the importance of teacher leadership explained to your staff and how do you encourage some of your teachers to start down this path? The third research question is blunt, and it was meant to be. We wanted to know if any of our respondents had a quality recruitment plan developed that we could share with the readers.

Research Question: How is the importance of teacher leadership communicated to stakeholders?

At this point readers might be asking themselves a couple of questions. The first is, "Isn't this communication piece a part of the recruitment process?" The answer, quite simply, is that we think it is. So important that we sought to discover exactly how this communication process works in school systems across the country. Similar to quality teachers being unaware that they are using best practices, we hypothesized those quality administrators might not be aware that they are communicating the importance of teacher leadership without even knowing it. The research question forced them to think not only about their methods of communication, but also whether they were discussing teacher leadership and not just leadership in general.

The second question the reader might be asking is, "shouldn't this communication piece occur much sooner than the third phase?" We think it should. Although certainly a part of the recruitment phase, the importance of teacher leadership should be communicated to teachers and all stakeholders soon after Phase 1, Realize. Some might argue that this should take place during the Realization Phase. Nevertheless, communicating the importance of teacher leadership and all its merits should occur before recruiting teacher leaders.

An added benefit of extolling the merits of teacher leadership early on is that it might get some of your teachers to think about the possibilities of their involvement in leadership positions that might not have happened otherwise. It also provides you with a nice segue when you begin to encourage those teachers with the characteristics and skills (Phase 2) needed to think more seriously about teacher leadership.

Furthermore, it is important that early on and throughout the recruitment process, the school administrators seek feedback and input (two-way communication) from stakeholders about the vision for teacher leadership and the recruitment process. By involving stakeholders in the process of establishing the vision for teacher leadership, they are more likely to support and be engaged in growing a culture of shared leadership in the school.

Our research indicates that the topic or concept of teacher leadership isn't discussed very often, and if it is, it is diluted to include components of educational leadership. A common response to this research question was, "Quite honestly, it isn't . . . at least not enough." One respondent reported, "We don't talk about it much, it has become an assumption or expectation of teaching duties." Another commented, "This is a weakness for us. We have not done much of this other than show casing good staff in our PR." And finally, one administrator stated, "I don't think we communicate it enough nor provide any incentive for teacher leadership."

It became apparent that some, but not many, respondents were well versed on the topic of teacher leadership and made it an integral part of their school's operations. "Teacher leadership has become a part of our school's culture. There are a variety of opportunities provided to staff and is has become a formal part of their annual performance plan." Our ultimate goal would be for each school district to be in a situation in which the administration would respond to this question as one of our respondents did,

> Teacher leadership needs to be a part of how the organization normally conducts business. It is evident in the structure of the school, the decisions that are made, the culture of the school and success of the school. You don't have to advertise it because it is how you operate and everyone can see that.

Many of our responses were similar to the following reply where the focus is on leadership, but not necessarily teacher leadership. "It is clearly articulated in our school leadership charter 'we are all leaders.'" Some respondents actually used the term *educational leader* in their answer, "In Australia we find ourselves in a situation where a huge percentage of educational leaders (baby boomers like me) are nearing retirement which will result in a potential leadership vacuum unless their replacements are supported and up-skilled."

Teacher leadership is different from educational (administrative) leadership. In Chapter 1, the reader is introduced to the *Nine Characteristics of High-Performing Schools*, developed by the Washington Department of Public Instruction (Appendix B). We believe that after careful examination of this chart, the difference between educational (administrative) and teacher leadership will become obvious.

In our experience, we have had many staff members who came to us with administrative aspirations, but few who had teacher leader aspirations. What we did discover, though, was that the more we discussed teacher leadership to staff members, we had more and more teachers warm to the concept. Some teachers began looking at themselves as a teacher leader rather than only a teacher. As a part of our Recruitment Plan, we make it clear that the focus and the message sent to staff members at the outset is on teacher leadership rather than leadership in general.

Research Question: How are teachers encouraged to become teacher leaders?

The act of encouraging a teacher to consider transitioning into a teacher leadership role is definitely a part of the recruitment process. Similar to the preceding question, many of our respondents seemed to group leadership and teacher leadership together, which further supports our contention that when leadership is mentioned or communicated to potential teacher leaders, it is important that administrators are able to articulate precisely what teacher leadership is. In our experience, any time we have the opportunity to discuss leadership (in general) to a group of teachers is constructive.

We make it a point to make certain our audience understands that what we are discussing are teacher leadership opportunities and the skills associated with such opportunities. We use words like *facilitate*, *advocate*, and *modeling* in these conversations so that the recipients come to understand that the type of leadership we are describing might be a little different from what they had experienced before.

We were encouraged by many of the responses that we received, like this one,

> We are just starting to implement teacher leaders in my school. It's not perfect, but we ask teachers to submit an application of interest in becoming a teacher leader. We provide a brief definition, but then ask them to provide their own definition and vision for what a teacher leader means to them.

This response is encouraging because it highlights the fact that often-new forms of leadership are messy, have kinks, but ultimately can lead to a transformative school culture. Like other practitioners, we find that teacher leadership, at first, may challenge even the best organizational structures and systems. However, through communication, transparency, gaining an understanding of what teacher leadership is and is not, school administrators, teachers, and schools grow a culture of teacher leadership that best fits their school.

Two emerging themes within this research question were judgment and support. Many respondents stated that their potential teacher leaders were provided with opportunities for their opinions and suggestions to be heard. One administrator asserted, "They are given a voice. They helped create our new vision at BJHS and they helped establish our 7 core values we expect our kids, faculty and staff to typify." Another respondent claimed, "Teacher input is sought in any meaningful change we make."

One respondent, who clearly trusts the judgment of his teachers claimed, "All teachers are encouraged to identify projects or initiatives they would like to lead, co-lead, learn more about or take responsibility for." Encouraging a culture of teacher leadership requires school administrators who embrace a culture of shared leadership, are not afraid to take risks, and are innovative in their approach to encourage collaboration and grow other leaders.

In our estimation, any administrator can encourage or provide opportunities for teachers to do more things, think outside the box, or attend professional training to learn more about a topic or concept. It was encouraging to discover how many of our respondents mentioned support in their responses. One respondent commented that it was their responsibility to, "Encourage and support teachers to contribute and develop their strengths and areas of expertise or areas they would like to professionally develop."

Another suggests, "Encouragement is demonstrated through open positive support for aspiring leaders and teachers prepared to 'step up.'" One administrator summed it up nicely by maintaining, "Listen to their concerns and suggestions, support them, and then give them the power to carry out the suggestions."

There were actually a few responses that gave an indication that the administrator had specific responsibilities in mind for his teacher leaders. This was not only a nice segue into the fifth phase (Nurture), but also clearly demonstrated that some were beyond merely talking or discussing teacher leadership, and were ready to take action. One administrator commented, "They are provided with the opportunity to represent our school or their team on school or district committees, attend professional learning and redeliver training, serve on school's leadership team, and propose schedules and solutions to challenging situations."

Another segue into the Nurture phase was provided by the following respondent who we thought summed it up nicely by asserting, "It takes patience in knowing there is a process in developing leaders, and the ability to help put others, and the commitment to allowing others to become better."

Research Question: What are the major components of your recruitment plan for teacher leaders? .

It wasn't surprising to us to discover that most of our respondents did not have a recruitment plan for teacher leaders. We theorized that many would have some type of recruitment plan much like the hypothesized plan from the second research question, but not one exclusively for teacher leaders. We had one response that not only summarized most of our responses but also highlighted the major theme running throughout, "We don't have a recruitment plan. If we want to have a teacher 'step up' we will just ask them personally." The personal approach to recruiting potential teacher leaders was mentioned by the majority of our respondents. Our research reaffirmed our original recommendation that this type of recruitment be a little more personal in nature (see our recommendations below).

One of our respondents stated, "I rely on self-identification and developing professional mentoring relationships with prospective teacher leaders." Another asserted, "Getting to know staff strengths and weaknesses, sending staff to selected professional development opportunities and having individual conversations about goals and next steps in their educational careers." Similarly, another responded, "Having one on one conversations with certain teachers several times a year and careful recruitment of new teachers leaders who seem to be 'healthy risk takers.'" Finally, this administrator, much like the preceding respondent, seemed to capture the spirit of both the second and third phases,

> Typically, teacher leaders emerge with a certain skillset that include the ability to influence others, respected knowledge of teaching and learning, the ability to articulate clearly, and a climate of trust with colleagues. When I recognize these traits, I typically invite the individual(s) to become involved in situations that capitalize on that skillset.

Our recommended recruitment plan is as follows. This plan uses elements of what we gleaned from our research and also, keeping with a distributive leadership theme, involves others in the process.

- Realize that teacher leaders are needed;
- Form a team, an advisory council to help throughout the recruitment process;
- Perform a needs assessment early in the process to recognize the need for teacher leaders and the necessary skills, characteristics, and experiences they need to possess;
- Communicate the opportunity to become a teacher leader and the purpose of teacher leadership to all staff members;
- Perform fieldwork to find the "right" individual to become a teacher leader;
- Recruit teachers to become leaders who possess the skills necessary to succeed and who will be compatible with the school administration;
- Personally converse with prospective teacher leaders, get to know who the teacher is and his or her goals and vision for the position;
- Make a decision about who to appoint or promote, based on skills, experiences, characteristics, potential, and compatibility; and
- Recognize the teacher leader to show full support not only for the individual, their new role, but also for teacher leadership in general.

VIGNETTE

Ms. Tonya Lighthouse is the second-year principal of PS 456 Elementary School. Ms. Lighthouse is recognized not only for her leadership, but also for her organization and communication skills. So, it should come as no surprise that when she began to grow teacher leaders, the process was effectively organized and well documented.

PS 456 Elementary School's Recruitment Plan for Teacher Leaders was not lengthy, but simple and transparent. Unlike in many schools, teacher leaders are recruited from within the school and in some cases recruited from other schools (inside and outside of the school district). The recruitment plan starts with clear and transparent description of the skills needed by the teacher leader. Ms. Lighthouse uses her school's principal advisory council to identify the skills needed. Furthermore, the principal advisory council is also responsible for develop the description for the position.

Though the description for teacher leaders is not posted to invite teachers to apply for the teacher leadership position, the description will be helpful later in the process. Ms. Lighthouse, once the description of teacher leaders is developed, leads the recruitment of teachers to be leaders. As she begins meeting with and observing prospective teacher leaders, Ms. Lighthouse uses the description developed by the school's principal advisory council to help her focus on finding teachers who meet the school's needs, stakeholder needs, as well as, can assist her in leading the school. She truly uses the input of others to find and recruit teacher leaders, but she also is cognizant of the fact that she must recruit teacher leaders who share her vision for the school and are compatible with her type of leadership.

Throughout the process of recruiting teacher leaders, Ms. Lighthouse continues to refer back to the role description developed by her advisory council. She communicates to prospective teacher leaders the importance of teacher leaders at PS 456 Elementary School. Ms. Lighthouse understands the importance of involving others in developing the vision for teacher leadership, as well as, communicating the vision for teacher leadership throughout the recruitment process. Two pillars for the recruitment plan at PS 456 Elementary School are communication and stakeholder involvement in determining the direction of teacher leadership.

PHASE 3 RECRUITMENT RECOMMENDATIONS

This portion of the chapter can be used as a checklist for the practicing administrator. Contained within this section are our recommendations for administrators who are using this book as a guide for growing teacher leaders. We also believe the concepts or ideas listed characterize each phase. We feel it is imperative that the following be completed or (in the works) before moving on to the next chapter.

Prior to our addressing our recommendations we would like to make the reader aware of a few things. First of all, the work that you have done promoting and publicizing teacher leadership up to this point may have "flown under the radar," so to speak. True action is called for during the Recruitment Phase. What we mean by this is you will be seen doing certain things that you haven't done previously. Secondly, don't be surprised if some of the non-recruits begin asking questions.

You have not made it a secret that you are more than interested in developing teacher leaders and have publicized this reality in a variety of different ways up to this point. Quite possibly, during this phase, you have noticed grumblings from the teaching staff that "something is up." In our experience, you will be notified of these grumblings by a lone representative, probably a member of the grumbling delegation. We would use this occasion as an opportunity to explain the benefits of distributive leadership in general and teacher leadership explicitly. And the answer to their questions usually ended with "yes, there are certain teachers who will be assuming a teaching and leadership role in the not too distant future."

Get Out There

What we mean by this is that to have an understanding of who your potential candidates are, it is important to see them in action. Some administrators get so caught up in the day-to-day operations of running the school or district that they rarely leave their office. Think of this as the administrator being a head basketball coach. Where does player evaluation occur? Where does the coaching occur? It happens during the game. The game of education is played in the classroom and also in the various meeting rooms. Our recommendation is to schedule time in your busy week to get in the classrooms and see your potential candidates in action. Try to schedule time to attend teacher meetings (professional learning community, curriculum, individualized education program) and a host of other meetings to see your potential candidates in situations outside the classroom. Get out in the hallway during passing time. Our experience has taught us that your candidates are out there talking with the students instead of holing themselves in their classrooms.

Furthermore, look for opportunities to watch potential teacher leaders engage with other teachers, staff members, parents, and students. One key to be an effective teacher leader is the ability to form relationships. School administrators must observe these relationships in action. Teacher leaders who are unable to form relationships with stakeholders will surely be determined to be ineffective.

Team Approach versus Individual Approach

In *The Leader Within*, we made the following comment about administrators,

> It has been said that administrators get paid the "big bucks" because it
> is they that have to have difficult conversations with some of their
> teachers. These difficult conversations often focus on teaching deficien-
> cies that need to be corrected. If they are not, termination is a likely
> conclusion. (p. 103)

We recommend (implied in our first recommendation) that you consider
taking time to discuss leadership opportunities to potential candidates on
your own. This is much different than the hypothetical set forth by the
recruitment process mentioned where a team approach is used throughout the process. An advisory council can be a great asset when exploring
the skills needed and developing a description of what the work of the
teacher leader candidate will entail. The final selection(s) and personal
conversation about the appointment should come from the administrator.

Our experience has taught us that selecting potential teacher leaders is
second only to selecting teaching candidates. Furthermore, selecting the
"right" teacher leader is just as important as selecting the "right" principal for the school. Just as superintendents look for school administrators
who possess the "right" experiences, skillset, and personality for the
principalship, administrators must also use the same understanding of
selecting the "right" teacher leader. This is accomplished by first communicating the expectations, the vision, and interaction and observation of
the prospective teacher leader.

Though, we still believe there are instances of "organic" growth of
teacher leadership in schools, the vast majority of teacher leadership is
intentional and strategically planned. We also believe that because you
are taking on this important responsibility on your own (so very different
from the typical team approach), teachers and administrators alike will
understand how vital teacher leadership is to you and your school.

The recruitment of teacher leaders must be somewhat personal for
school administrators. The partnership between school administrators
and teacher leaders must be solid, in other words, compatible and rewarding for each side. School administrators are recruiting teachers to be
leaders to assist in leading the school; therefore, they must be able together and have the same goals, dedication, and vision for the school and
student success.

Begin Thinking About How to Encourage Teacher Leadership

It should be noted that one of our recommendations from Chapter 1
was to begin planting the teacher leadership seeds. Encouraging takes

your commitment to teacher leadership to a whole new level. The main difference between planting and encouraging is when planting, you cast a wide net; when you encourage, you begin to individualize the conversations you have with those teachers who possess the characteristics inherent in teacher leaders.

We contend that the process of growing and developing teacher leadership is done intentionally. As former administrators, we have always had those who stepped up to the plate and volunteered to be a part of the variety of committees initiated each and every year. We came to appreciate these staff members for their willingness to pitch in and help in the hiring process, be members of a curriculum selection committee, or supervise during extracurricular activities. But do these volunteers have the resilience and determination to oversee your professional learning community process at your school? Teacher leadership goes beyond mere volunteering. In fact, teacher leaders want opportunities to formally lead, whether coaching and mentoring teachers, facilitating and leading professional learning communities, leading the various school committees, or being part of the school's leadership team.

If you were able to check off these three recommendations, then you are well on your way to developing teacher leaders in your school or district. If not, what steps can be made right now to address those unchecked?

KEY TAKEAWAYS

The key takeaways are components that each administrator or aspiring teacher leader must understand to grow and develop teacher leaders in his or her building or district. Additionally, the section allows for readers to identify their own key takeaways from Phase 3. This is a way to reflect on your learning to grow teacher leadership or to develop as a teacher leader.

- The recruitment process for teacher leaders is unique from the typical recruitment process most schools adhere to.
- The recruitment process begins with discussing teacher leadership with all stakeholders. It is imperative that the administrator focus on teacher leadership (characteristics and skills) and not general leadership.
- It is recommended that administrators observe potential candidates in action in many different situations.
- Most school districts do not have a recruitment plan for teacher leaders.
- Most administrators personally select those considered worthy of a leadership position.

- As Ms. Lighthouse did, involve stakeholders in the recruitment process by allowing them to be involved in developing the vision for teacher leadership.
- Perform a teacher leadership needs assessment before beginning the recruitment process to identify the skillset, talents, experiences, and such, that prospective teacher leaders need to have to be effective in a particular school.

List Your Own Takeaways in the Space Provided

_____

_____

_____

_____

CHAPTER SUMMARY

As we discovered through our research, the recruitment phase of teacher leadership is often overlooked or discounted as a process that can be skipped. But in fact, the effectiveness of the recruitment process and plan is a key determinant of the overall effectiveness of teacher leadership in your school. If you appoint or promote the wrong teacher to be a leader in the school, he or she will ultimately be ineffective and possibly have a negative effect on the school's culture, processes, student achievement and the school's leadership capacity.

However, if the "right" teacher is appointed or promoted to be a leader, great things happen for students, teachers, leadership, and the school community.

Taking the time to develop a strategic recruitment plan will lead to positive net gains in several areas. Though a teacher leader recruitment plan may not exist in your school, we recommend that you take the time to develop one. Recruiting teacher leaders must be strategic and well planned. Though school administrators may struggle finding time to develop a recruitment plan, we encourage throughout this chapter to form an advisory council to help relieve the burden and time constraints to recruiting teacher leaders.

Just as we have stressed countless times up to this point and in *The Leader Within*, school leadership must be shared, distributed, and collaborative, which is only more reason to engage others in developing an effective recruitment plan aligned to the needs of the school and the school's vision. The final selection(s) and personal conversation about the appointment should come from the administrator. Finally, it is important that the school administration recognize teacher leaders not only after they have been appointed to the position, but as often as possible. Consistently recognizing teacher leaders will help improve the recruitment process when it must be used again.

FOUR

Phase 4: Grow Leadership Capabilities Among Teachers

The first step to growing teacher leaders is ensuring that the school's culture is characterized by learning. A culture of learning leads to a focus on student achievement and the development of staff. A culture of learning also helps to grow leadership capacity. One of our respondents, who obviously has experience growing teacher leaders, exemplified not only the journey to the Growth phase, but why teacher leadership is important in the first place.

Administrators need to provide opportunities for teachers to lead and can do so in a variety of ways. Giving them the opportunity to present in front of their colleagues can be a start. Also placing them in positions where they can assume more responsibility such as building or district leadership teams. Furthermore, administrators need to share leadership

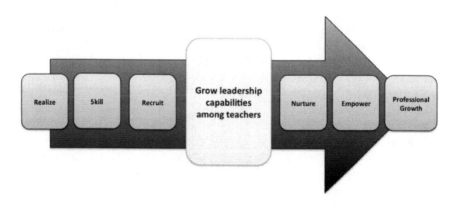

Figure 4.1.

to build capacity and extend the scope of leadership to include nurturing and mentoring teacher leaders.

At this stage in our process, the administrator and their leadership team have successfully identified potential teacher leaders in your school and the individual conversations have been had with those select few. Our experience has taught us that sometimes, even the best laid plans go to waste at times. No doubt, some of the high flyers you had your eye on turned down the request and have decided to stay in the classroom, happy and content to focus on developing their teaching skills. The focus now shifts to growing or building leadership capabilities among those that remain.

At this point in the book, readers might be asking themselves, "What is the difference between growing and nurturing?" "How quickly will my new recruits move through each phase?" These are questions that we have asked ourselves numerous times, but in our experience, it is important to remain patient. As one respondent so eloquently suggested, "It takes patience in knowing there is a process in developing teacher leaders, and the commitment to allow others to become better." Some may feel the need to jump to Phase 6 and empower these new teacher leaders with responsibilities and duties they are not ready for. Our recommendation is to ease them into their new positions and make the transition period as rewarding and worthwhile as you possibly can.

During this transition period or Phases 4 to 6 (Grow, Nurture, and Empower) you might have some teacher leaders who transition through these phases more rapidly than others. We have stated many times before, each district is unique in the sense that the characteristics and skills needed in one district might not be true for another. Just as each district is unique, so too will be your newly recruited teacher leaders.

Some might breeze through Phases 4 and 5, whereas some might need to spend a little more time in each, honing their skills. A word to the wise, don't expect all of them to evolve and transition at the same rate. If you did your due diligence, and carefully selected those with certain characteristics or dispositions to be teacher leaders, most will be at the same point, in this regard, at the beginning of Phase 4.

As we stressed in Chapter 2, some may be more skilled than others and that's okay. Your job is to allow those that are more skilled to develop and move through Phases 4 and 5 as speedily as you see fit. Much like those high flyers in the classroom that completed the assignments so quickly that they needed enrichment exercises, you may find yourself ill-prepared for how quickly some take to their new assignments, so be prepared. Our recommendation is for you to focus on those that need more guidance and support and let your team members focus on the high flyers.

We also wanted to stress the lens through which we viewed each of these phases. In Bolman and Deal's *Reframing Organizations* (2013), we are taught about the usage of frames or lenses through which individuals view organizations. The authors describe a lens as something used to focus and filter some things out and allow others to pass through. The lens helps individuals order experience. The best analogy we can think of comes from the world of coaching. The lens a parent uses to view a situation (son not playing in the game) is much different from that of the coach (who knows the son is not skilled enough to keep up with the level of play on the floor). The lens through which we view Growing and Nurturing is couched in teacher leadership and the Teacher Leader Model Standards (TLMS).

Before moving on to the next section of Phase 4, we think it wise to offer our definitions of Growing and Nurturing (through the lens of developing teacher leaders) and what each might entail. As educational researchers, leaders, and practitioners we have developed our understanding through experiences. These experiences have caused us to view growing and nurturing teacher leaders as separate phases that we believe only strengthen the result. We realize that each reader may or may not have experience with teacher leadership, but either way, we present the results from our research and our understandings as a way to only help develop this uniquely strategic process.

Growing

Growing teacher leaders is the process of allowing teacher leaders to develop and acquire the skills necessary to be successful. Growing is all about presenting opportunities for your newly recruited teacher leader, that is, a series of learning opportunities or single events that assist the teacher leader to understand leadership and their new role within the school. These growth opportunities are personalized to meet the needs of the teacher leader and aligned to specific skills and needs within the district. Growth is also a time for experimentation and trial and error.

During the Growing phase, it is possible not all of your recruits will find success. Though you may view this as a failure on your part, it is not; not everyone can be a leader and it is better to recognize that now before moving them into the nurture and empowerment phases. Once the skills that must be possessed by teacher leaders have been identified, the school administrator must begin to help the teacher leader grow those particular skills. For instance, if communication is a skill the teacher leader must be taught, the growth opportunities must include opportunities for teacher leaders to hone their communication skills.

Like other researchers and practitioners, we believe that leadership can be learned, and therefore, grown. According to the Center for Creative Leadership (2015) leadership skills are grown through a 70:20:10 Leadership Development Process. Within the model, prospective leaders are grown by providing them 70 percent challenging assignments, 20 percent development relationships, and 10 percent actual training program. This model validates our belief that teacher leaders are not merely grown through opportunity but through a strategic process.

Nurturing

Nurturing teacher leaders is the process of continued/ongoing mentorship and coaching by school administrators. Nurturing is the continued support of school administrators to fine-tune the skills and strategies teacher leaders learned or acquired throughout the growth process. As stated in the growing definition, the trial-and-error period is over. At this juncture, your newly recruited teacher leaders should be showing promise. A crucial matter that will be discussed in greater detail in Chapter 5 is your role in the process of assisting teacher leaders to remain interested and engaged in leadership. This can only be done by assisting teacher leaders to overcome obstacles and barriers that may derail their leadership journey.

Finally, teacher leaders must experience success and develop the skills to overcome failures and remove barriers. School administrators are critical mentors and coaches throughout the nurturing phase as teacher leaders acquire and develop skills necessary to be successful in their roles.

PULSE CHECK

- How much time should your teacher leaders spend in the Growth Phase? Do all of your new recruits have the same characteristics and skills?
- How do you determine that you have chosen the wrong person to assume a leadership position in your school?
- How long do your new teacher leaders remain in the Growth phase? What are some accomplishments that inform you that they are ready to move into the Nurture phase?
- What are the necessary skills your new recruits must develop prior to the Empowerment stage?

RESEARCH QUESTIONS AND EXPLANATION OF FINDINGS

The two questions that guided our research during this phase were:

1. How do you allow for experimentation and learning, followed by repeated practice for your teacher leaders?
2. How are teachers provided opportunities to learn and develop skills needed to be school leaders?

Readers should be reminded about our research methodology before moving forward. A different group of administrators were asked each question. It is obvious that both questions are related, and that was done intentionally. Our assumption was that the responses to question one would focus on opportunities. We wanted to discover exactly what type of opportunities they were allowed to experience and learn from. The second question, although similar to the first question, required the respondent to think about how these opportunities were created. What we discovered in our research were not only many different opportunities, but also something that goes much deeper.

It is what you discern through observations and conversations about your teacher leaders through these many opportunities that may be more important than the opportunities themselves. We assert that the opportunities you provide your teacher leaders might be infinite, the what is not. We knew, through our experiences, that not all—even those recruits who possess the crucial characteristics—will find success. We wanted to delve into this topic as well during the Growth phase, but knew that examining this piece is difficult when using a survey. We intentionally added it as one of our follow-up research questions.

Research Question: How do you allow for experimentation and learning, followed by repeated practice for your teacher leaders?

As we stated previously, we expected to get many responses to this research question that mentioned providing opportunities. For many researchers, it is when they stumble upon the unexpected that provide them with the greatest satisfaction. While researching this phase, one unquestionable truth was stated by many of the respondents, the Growth phase is when it is okay to take risks. One of our respondents asserted, "We encourage and model an atmosphere of risk taking without fear of consequences."

Another suggests that during this phase it is important to "promote an ethos of risk taking, innovation and deep self-reflection." As you recall, (risk-taking) was one of the many characteristics or dispositions mentioned in Chapter 2. It was refreshing to read so many respondents claim that risk-taking is not only a disposition, but something that should be stressed to teacher leaders during this very important phase. We believe this administrator put it best, "We encourage risk taking but demand accountability. We continually ask, 'How do you know you had an impact?'"

Another aspect of our research in this phase was the importance most administrators placed on personal goal setting. One respondent asserted, "Teacher leaders set goals and design their own next steps in a supportive environment." Another administrator looked at this phase as a time to "review their goals and make adjustments if needed." Many used the words *growth mind-set* in their responses. For example, "We encourage and expect emergent leaders to set goals, participate, and actively engage. We are trying to use a growth mindset in all levels of the organization." Our research suggests that many administrators believe growth mind-set to be a part of Phase 5, Nurture, and it will be examined in greater detail in Chapter 5.

The opportunities that you provide your teacher leaders during the Growth phase will be unique for your school or district. Searby and Shaddix (2008) posit, "Schools in which teachers are becoming significant leaders have structures in place that provide opportunities for broad participation in teams, study groups, vertical communities, and action research teams" (p. 1). One respondent in our research stated, "Opportunities to be involved in a variety of programs or projects, with support that is progressively reduced."

This administrator no doubt understood that you can't coddle your new recruits forever, but they will need some added attention early on. Another administrator asserts, "I look for leadership opportunities and put them on essential committees. If I see a teacher leader exceeding expectations, I plant seeds and encourage them to be a part of one of the school-wide leadership teams."

Some of the most prevalent opportunities we collected are listed here. Each and every one would no doubt provide the teacher leader with a platform to develop their skills. One respondent asserted,

> I strive to have all teachers involved in some part of running the campus. Whether it is leading staff development or a book study, building campus morale or leading after school programs for students, I want them all involved in some leadership role.

This administrator listed many quality opportunities, but how many are explicit to building teacher leaders? We can't stress enough that it isn't good enough to provide opportunities that develop conventional leadership skills. In Chapter 2, we listed specific teacher leadership skills that were derived from our current research and also those skills identified in the TLMS. A short summary of these skills are listed here.

Teaching/Instruction	Communication	Big Picture
Listening	Relationships	Collaboration
Organization	Facilitation	Advocacy
Modeling	Research	Reflection
Adult Learning Theory		

The *italicized* opportunities are those that we believe are most appropriate during the Growth phase. They are considered most appropriate because we believe they encompass many of the teacher leader skills delineated in Chapter 2.

1. *Professional Learning Communities (PLCs)*
2. Book (or article) study
3. District policy evaluation team
4. Shadowing program
5. Action research project
6. *Leading discussions*
7. *Deliver presentation from teacher or leadership conference*
8. Involvement in a (pilot) program
9. Staff development
10. *Campus climate team*

Similar to our experience discovering (creating a risk-free environment and growth mind-set) mentioned previously, another finding during our research of this phase was that the teacher leaders were becoming more resourceful and innovative. One respondent avowed, "The teacher leaders understand that it's okay to fail at something. We just try again in a different, more innovative way." Although difficult to prove, we believe innovation is a by-product of creating a risk-taking environment.

Teacher leaders in this stage should, after experiences and time, not be the same person they were when they began. They should be evolving, if you will. Although these concepts are difficult to quantify, they were listed enough times by our respondents that we knew they needed to be included. Finally, an administrator stated it quite bluntly, "I give them the green light unless it's dangerous, against the law, or if funding does not allow. It is encouraging to see them seek out other resources."

Research Question: How are teachers provided opportunities to learn and develop skills needed to be school leaders?

One of the things we came to appreciate during our research was the honesty and candor of some of our respondents. In answering this research question, one administrator stated, "Tap their God given talents and give them responsibilities on campus." This wasn't exactly what we were hoping to find, but sometimes a little levity is a good thing. We soon realized that our two research questions were so similar that our respondents focused on the opportunities rather than the how, which is what we were hoping to discover. Many of the opportunities generated from the first question were restated in the responses to this research question. Although we did not discover any emerging themes, we did find some responses that indicated what some schools are doing to provide opportunities to grow teacher leaders.

It was refreshing to find many of the responses were firmly grounded in Phase 4 (growth mentality). Obviously, each respondent had recruited a group of potential teacher leaders and describes how his school or district has created their unique teacher leader niche. One of our respondents affirmed, "We jointly created a teacher leadership cohort with our teachers union." Another respondent commented, "Through two-hour teacher leaders forums held three times per term."

Finally, this administrator sought support outside the district, joining forces with a higher education institution. "We had a great relationship with an institution of higher learning that contributed to the professional development side of things. They provided instructional coaching, cognitive coaching, mentoring, induction, and leadership training to our candidates." However you decide to create your teacher leader niche will be unique to your school or district.

It is important that "opportunity" to grow the skills necessary to be an effective teacher leader is as close to real situations that the prospective teacher leader will experience as a school leader. The "opportunity" should be an actual opportunity—not short amounts of time. Consider providing prospective teacher leaders opportunities that may be 1 to 3 days in length. The Growth phase is such an important process that we recommend not skimping with the amount of time teacher leaders are given to grow, develop, and acquire the skills to be effective in their position.

VIGNETTE

Dr. Middleton is principal of East Town Middle School. East Town Middle School is considered one of the best middle schools in the district and in the region. The school regularly has high student performance, teacher effectiveness ratings, high parent, and community engagement. The school's ongoing success is attributed to a culture of stakeholder empowerment and shared leadership. The school has seen remarkable improvement and transformation because of the school's commitment to growing leadership skills in stakeholders, particularly teachers.

The transformation that has occurred at East Town Middle School is truly a testament to growing leadership capacity. Dr. Middleton has been successful at establishing a culture of learning and growth through creating a process to growing teacher leaders. The process to growing teacher leaders at East Town Middle School includes developing the skills the prospective teacher leaders possess, while also helping them grow new skills that are needed by the school, students, and other stakeholders. The growth and development of teacher leaders involves several key processes that many school leaders seek to replicate in their schools. Many school leaders from other schools from within the district and in the region often visit East Town Middle School to observe the process of growing teacher leaders.

The growth process of teacher leaders at East Town Middle School has two basic principles: a formalized training program and action learning experiences through school-based opportunity. The state's association of school administrators and teachers' association are partners in the state's program that offers leadership development for teachers. East Town Middle School is afforded several seats per year to send teachers to the leadership development program. Each year, several prospective teacher leaders are given an opportunity to develop their leadership skills in a formalized program taught by leading researchers and practitioners from the state's colleges, universities, and schools. The formalize program's components include: leadership readiness assessment, leadership focus areas, and a 1-year mentorship from a highly effective school leader.

The second principle that forms the teacher leadership development at East Town Middle School includes real learning experiences. Working closely with the school's advisory council, Dr. Middleton organizes key learning opportunities for each prospective teacher leader. The learning opportunities are based on the skills of the teacher, data from the leadership readiness assessment from the formalized program, and the needs of the school. The opportunities are strategic and closely aligned to the school's vision and vision for teacher leadership.

The keys to East Town Middle School's success with developing teacher leaders, as Dr. Middleton has repeatedly stated, are partnerships with educational institutions and organizations, strategic planning, and real-life experiences. If a teacher wants to be a leader at East Town Middle School, Dr. Middleton says, the teacher leader is going to be trained, engage in an internship-style learning experience, coupled with coaching and mentorship.

PHASE 4 GROWTH RECOMMENDATIONS

At this juncture, there are many (maybe not many, but certainly some) changes occurring in your school. No doubt, most inquiring minds have noticed some among their ranks being asked to be involved with committee work, being sent to conferences, and possibly even speaking about topics considered (administrative) at the most recent faculty meeting. You might even be asked a simple question that if not considered deeply, could make or break your design for building a collaborative culture based on teacher leadership. That question is, "What is your plan?" The section about Long-Term Planning is directly related to this matter.

You need to know what the end game is for your new recruits. Bierly, Doyle, and Smith (2016) contend that although huge investments are being made to develop leaders, there is rarely a plan in place to use these people effectively. Have a plan. Donaldson (2006) argues that one of the major shortcomings of the efforts to develop teacher leaders is uncertain or unclear authority. Be able to explain the type of authority or influence these new recruits will have. Choose your words wisely when expounding the virtues of teacher leadership and at the same time justifying that the only real authority lies with you. Teacher leaders are, after all, teachers.

Barth (2001) warns of a few challenges that the resourceful administrator is already aware. He suggests, "Inertia, risk aversion, lack of confidence, and primitive adult relationships all thwart teacher initiatives toward school leadership. Collectively, they provide a backdrop against which more active forms of resistance from teachers play out" (p. 446). Finally, Barth (2013) warns of trying to make changes in a leveling profession,

> Teachers are, in a way, their own worst enemy when it comes to unlocking leadership because they don't welcome it, typically don't respect it, and often feel threatened by one of their own taking it on. Anyone who bumps above the level is subject to condemnation: "Who the heck do you think you are?!" I'm not talking about trends—I'm talking about people impeding teacher leadership. Some of the people are called principals, and some are called teachers. (p. 10)

Long-Term Planning

The concept or idea that characterizes the Growth phase is opportunity. Teacher leaders during this phase should be given the opportunity to take risks, and we have found that in this sheltered environment, many teacher leaders prove their worth by being resourceful and innovative. The smart administrator is about two steps ahead of the game. What we mean by this, is by now you should have an idea what exactly it is you are going to have your new recruit(s) actually do in the Empower Phase. The challenge for the administrator is to skillfully create opportunities that encompass the skills they will need in their new position. The following example illustrates what we are getting at with this recommendation.

The administrator realizes that his school or district needs to enhance outreach efforts and collaboration with families and community (Domain 6: TLMS). The administrator knows that one of the new teacher leader recruits will be given the important responsibility of not only promoting, but also overseeing this outreach program. The skills needed to perform this task responsibly include research, facilitation, advocacy, leading discussions, and presenting ideas, to name a few. Placing this new recruit on a committee (e.g., Parent Teacher Organization) that hones these skills better prepares him or her for the future position he or she will hold when the Empowerment phase is reached.

Finally, Allio (2005) recommends the following when considering the type of opportunity created for your new recruits. "Leadership is dormant until possible leaders have the opportunity to display their mettle in specific situations. Leadership competence develops when an individual is forced to address the challenge of innovating, inspiring, and adapting" (p. 1074). We recommend that you look for opportunities that will challenge your new recruits.

KEY TAKEAWAYS

The key takeaways are components that each administrator or aspiring teacher leader must have to grow and develop teacher leaders in his or her building or district. Additionally, the section allows for readers to identify their own key takeaways from Phase 4. This is a way to reflect on your learning to grow teacher leadership or to develop as a teacher leader.

- Don't be discouraged if some of your teacher leader recruits turn down your efforts.
- Teacher leader recruits will transition through each phase at their own pace. Do not make the mistake of placing a time limit on (Growth) for your new recruits. Patience, flexibility, and time are of the essence during this phase.
- Growing teacher leaders is the process of allowing teacher leaders to develop and acquire the skills necessary to be successful.
- Nurturing teacher leaders is the process of continued or ongoing mentorship and coaching by school administrators.
- There are a variety of opportunities you can provide for your teacher leader recruits. It is imperative that these opportunities are tailored to develop specific teacher leader skills.
- Our research suggests that the Growth phase is characterized as a time when teacher leader recruits are encouraged to take risks.
- Administrators may notice their recruits becoming more resourceful and innovative during the Growth phase.
- How you create your teacher leader niche is unique in relation to other districts. There is no one-size-fits-all approach.

List Your Own Takeaways in the Space Provided

_____

_____

_____

_____

CHAPTER SUMMARY

As school administrators begin the process to grow teacher leaders, they must ensure that the school's culture is characterized by learning and collaboration. A culture of learning leads to a focus on student achievement and the development of staff. A culture of learning helps to grow leadership capacity. Effectively growing teacher leaders requires school administrators to provide new recruits with opportunities to actively engage in learning experiences that are aligned with the specific teacher leader skills and the district's strategic plan. It is important that teacher leaders understand how their growth fits in the school's strategic plan.

According to Searby and Shaddix (2008), "Growing teacher leaders needs to be an intentional act in our nation's school systems. Principals nearing retirement must prepare to pass the torch of leadership to those who come after them; those who will carry the torch in the future are the classroom room teachers of today" (p. 1). Growing teacher leaders is an active process whereby teachers learn and grow skills necessary to lead by engaging in real school experiences, under the direction of school administrators.

Teacher leaders in this phase need the autonomy to develop skills based on the needs of the school and through specifically designed opportunities that develop these skills. Their growth is not a destination, but a journey. Teacher leaders need to develop skills that will aide them in their growth well beyond their appointment to a leadership position within the school. Furthermore, they must model this commitment to a life of learning for others because they will have others who look to them for leadership and mentoring.

School leaders must allocate time and resources to growing teacher leaders. Effectively growing teacher leaders requires patience and no shortcuts. School leaders must have a focus on the learning experiences and opportunities for teacher leaders, ensuring alignment to effectively preparing them for their new roles. It is important not to become discouraged throughout the process because it may seem like a daunting task.

Keep in mind that you are growing teacher leaders to ensure student success and grow the depth of the leadership bench in your school. As schools continue to increase in complexities, teacher leaders will be essential leaders who can work side by side with school administrators to help remain focused on student success and the school's overall vision.

FIVE

Phase 5: Nurture Leadership Qualities in Teachers

As we stated in Chapter 4, the terms *grow* and *nurture* are sometimes used synonymously. We believe that in teacher leadership development, there is a difference and our research substantiates our claim. Throughout the Growth phase, the teacher leader recruits were given numerous opportunities to demonstrate their worth and, depending on the situation, were able to prove themselves creditable candidates for a leadership position in your school. Not to let "the cat out of the bag" or jump too far ahead in our analysis, but the next phase (Phase 6) is empowerment.

Some of these teacher leader recruits will be put in charge of something in the not too distant future. They have proven that they possess the skills and characteristics requisite of teacher leaders. They have strategically been given opportunities to hone their skills during the Growth

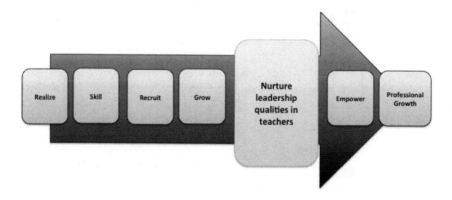

Figure 5.1.

phase. Before putting them in charge of your curriculum review program, we believe, and our research confirms, that they need a personal touch.

PULSE CHECK

- How involved have you been in the process of developing teacher leaders up to this point?
- How often do you discuss the performance of teacher leaders with them individually?
- What is it that your recruited teacher leaders do or say that give you confidence that they will succeed during the Empowerment phase?

RESEARCH QUESTIONS AND EXPLANATION OF FINDINGS

The two questions that guided our research during this phase were:

1. What is the role of the school administrator in the development of the teacher leaders?
2. How do administrators nurture teacher leaders throughout the growth process?

We aren't sure if it is semantics or the way the questions were worded, but the vast majority of our respondents described what they did during this phase, which was much different from the responses from the Growth phase. It wasn't as if we just started asking questions that referenced the administrator's role or responsibility during this process. Many of our research questions used the words (*you* and *your*) that subconsciously might elicit a personal response, but for the most part, they didn't. For example, in response to our first research question in this phase, one of our respondents suggests, "I give them tasks that will stretch their abilities, challenge them, and I offer support through open dialogue."

At this phase, the majority of administrators individualized their role and stepped up their influence in nurturing their recruited teacher leaders. If you recall in Chapter 3, one of our recommendations was for the administrator to take a personal approach during the Recruitment phase. This individual approach will serve you well when nurturing your new teacher leaders.

Research Question: What is the role of the school administrator in the development of the teacher leaders?

The majority of the responses to our first research question were, in a word, predictable. One of our respondents stated, "School administrators should be serving as mentors and role models for potential teacher leaders." Referencing again to our research methodology, readers should be reminded that we sought out administrators who had experience working with teacher leaders. During the Nurture phase we anticipated responses that focused on mentorship, support, and guidance and our research reaffirmed our assumptions. It wasn't until we examined the second research question that we discovered how "personal" our respondents took their role in this process. ·

One interesting characteristic at this point in our research was how often the word *leadership* was used in response to these two research questions. It wasn't as if the word suddenly appeared in the responses, but it does constitute an emerging theme during this phase because of how frequently it was mentioned. For instance, one administrator asserted, "My role is to step aside at times to encourage leadership to happen." Another suggests, "Be willing to trust others to take on a leadership role and accept that some things may be done differently." Finally, "The most important component is to provide honest feedback and to engage in reflective conversations that help the teacher to critically analyze their own leadership."

We recommend that if you haven't already done so, it is the perfect time to begin discussing leadership in general, and leadership styles in particular, with your emerging teacher leaders. One could say that nurturing teacher leaders is like using "training wheels" to help teacher leaders to become comfortable leading, before riding a bike with little assistance.

A key responsibility of school administrators in the nurturing phase is to help teacher leaders to understand their role as a leader in the school, in other words, to connect the dots. Teacher leaders must understand how to use their skills to be more effective in their roles. Furthermore, school administrators must coach teacher leaders on how to use their skills and position to improve student achievement. Connecting the dots will help teacher leaders to align their work with the school's vision. The vision for teacher leadership must always be aligned to the school's vision.

Before moving on to the next research question, we feel it incumbent to reiterate something examined in Chapter 2. We believe it is imperative that when mentoring emerging teacher leaders it is important to focus on skills related to teacher leadership and not administration or educational leadership. Teacher leadership skills were examined at length in Chapter

2 and will again be explored in Chapter 7. Your focus should be on mentoring aspiring teacher leaders, not aspiring administrators.

We have both been asked to supervise the internship or practicum experience for aspiring administrators in the past. The prerequisites and requirements for emerging administrators are different than those espoused for teacher leaders. Once again, reexamine the skills your teacher leaders will need to do their jobs proficiently. We believe that you will realize the skills you use to be a successful administrator are not the same needed by your emerging teacher leaders.

Research Question: How do administrators nurture teacher leaders throughout the growth process?

First and foremost, we thought this research question would inform us about how administrators defined the word *nurture*. Little did we know this question would elicit so many responses about what they did personally with their evolving teacher leaders. The personal touch, more specifically, one-on-one conversations, was another major theme in the Nurture phase. One of our respondents summed up where we are in developing teacher leaders as,

> Knowing your teachers is key. Once I have a relationship built, we can have conversations that delve into their growth and learning. I support them in their learning as necessary, valuing their abilities and offering opportunities for them to take on responsibility without micromanaging helps.

One administrator commented, "I take time to chat about how things are going, support them and provide encouragement as needed." Keeping with the leadership theme examined previously, one administrator stated, "I discuss things with them about their leadership style." Another respondent asserted, "I provide honest feedback and engage in reflective conversations that help the teacher leader to critically analyze their own leadership and collaborate to determine ways to expand opportunities and enhance skills." Finally, one of our administrators affirmed, "I really get to know them, I give them tasks that will stretch their abilities, challenge them, and support them through open dialogue."

It would have been helpful if our research yielded details about what these personal conversations were about besides leadership, but it didn't. Many of our respondents reported how they offered encouragement and support. We firmly believe that our respondents explain things best, and although lengthy, the following comment about the administrative role sums up the Nurture phase aptly.

> Everyone takes a part to embrace, model and talk the language of self-improvement and growth, but the principal as a leading learner must create and ensure this climate is expected, maintained, contributed to

and celebrated. Nurturing growth includes a variety of planned and unplanned practices that may evolve but includes mentoring; coaching; the development and discussion of professional learning plans; providing challenges and encouragement and a belief in their capacities to lead and take the initiative to solve problems or improve practices to better support students' learning or the school culture.

We believe that nurturing, like growing, must be individualized to the specific needs of each teacher leader. This takes time. Time is a precious commodity for most administrators. As experienced school and district-based administrators we truly understand how valuable every second is, especially in today's educational climate. Though time is valuable, we encourage school administrators to schedule a block of time to personalize the nurturing of teacher leaders during this phase. Our recommendation is that this is done on a weekly basis.

VIGNETTE

Dr. Dailey is principal of Marshall High School, in a district with only three schools: the large high school, Marshall Elementary School, and Marshall Middle School. The stakeholders in the Marshall community are recognized for their support of education and the school district. Like the larger community, Dr. Dailey has worked tirelessly over the past 5 years to create a school culture that is supportive of teachers' professional growth.

Dr. Dailey has specifically focused on the professional growth of teacher leaders as he has come to realize their importance in long-term strategic planning at the school level. He and his team have implemented several key components in the school that have been recognized by teachers and teacher leaders. Many of the teacher leaders have commented that they would not be a teacher leader if had not been for Dr. Dailey's leadership and willingness to allow teachers to be leaders in the school. Additionally, they are very appreciative for his emphasis on offering teacher leaders coaching and mentoring throughout their leadership development process.

Unlike in many schools, Dr. Dailey has developed and implemented key nurturing components that go beyond just coaching and mentoring. One component that is somewhat different from others components that are typically found is the emphasis on the self-reflection of the teacher leader throughout the nurturing process. Dr. Dailey meets with each teacher leader weekly to discuss their self-reflection and growth. Through these conversations, Dr. Dailey and his leadership team can identify additional trainings needed and supports and resources that will aid in the growth of each individual teacher leader.

The key difference is the emphasis on self-reflection and offering strategic supports based on the self-reflection by teacher leaders. At Marshall High School, the nurturing of teacher leaders is strategic based largely on the self-reflection. Dr. Dailey understands the importance of helping aspiring leaders to identify their strengths and areas of growth by practicing self-reflection. By growing the skill and ability of teacher leaders to practice self-reflection he has been able to make the nurturing process more personalized and strategic.

As Dr. Dailey and his leadership team, including teacher leaders, have been able to grow a culture of teacher leadership and develop a highly effective leadership development program at Marshall High School, many of the components have migrated into other school processes. As a result of the successes experienced growing and empowering teacher leaders, Dr. Dailey has integrated personalized nurturing processes, based on regular self-reflection, into the new teacher induction program at Marshall High School. His leadership, vision, and focus on personalized development have truly transformed the school's culture, student achievement, and teacher and leadership performance. Furthermore, his focus on personalization has led to even greater engagement of stakeholders from the community.

PHASE 5 NURTURE RECOMMENDATIONS

Nurturing teacher leaders is tough for a variety of reasons. Finding time in your busy schedule, which was mentioned in previous chapters, is difficult enough. Nurturing teacher leaders is also beset by the "egalitarian nature" of teaching and one has to work hard to gain acceptance and respect (Hart, 1990; Lieberman, Saxl, & Miles, 1988; Wasley, 1989). Cultivating leadership in identified teachers often violates the "equal status" of teachers and can breed resentment and hostility toward teachers in leadership positions (Devaney, 1987; Hart, 1990; Wasley, 1989).

We firmly believe the nurturing phase is not a single step in the growth process, but it is actually a continuous process. It is important to realize how important nurturing is to developing, acquiring, and sustaining the skills necessary to be an effective teacher leader. Think about all of the skills that the teacher leader has developed or acquired up to this point in the process. If grown effectively, each of the skills mentioned in Chapter 4 are important and critical to the success of teacher leaders. To ensure success, it is important that the school's culture and environment is conducive to growing, learning, and nurturing. As mentioned previously, nurturing is tough, and the impetus to change the "egalitarian and equal" character that defines teaching starts with you.

We argue that the nurturing phase starts now but extends into the empowerment and professional learning phase. Nurturing is a journey and not a destination. It is important that school administrators work closely with teacher leaders to instill in them the understanding and belief that failure is a learning process. Throughout the nurturing process, teacher leaders will undoubtedly experience failures, obstacles, setbacks, and barriers; however, school administrators must be there to help them find solutions that will help them to continue their leadership journey and help the school continue to move forward.

As we have come to realize, often teacher leaders are not provided essential learning experiences whereby they develop the resolve to be leaders. We understand that teacher leaders are provided opportunities to develop the skills necessary to be effective, but we are concerned that they are not provided the opportunities to actually learn how to use the skills. The school administrator must practice patience throughout the nurturing phase. We understand how difficult it is not to solve their problem as teacher leaders experience obstacles, setbacks, and barriers. It is the responsibility of the school administrator to help the teacher leader to understand how to use these experiences as a means to polish their skills, as well as, to develop additional skills that may not have been acquired through the Growth phase.

Servant Leadership

One of the things that came out of our research was the need for the administrator to begin discussing types of leadership with their new recruits. We recommend that the majority of these conversations focus on servant leadership. Servant leadership is based on the premise that leaders who are best able to motivate followers are those who focus least on satisfying their own personal needs and most on prioritizing the fulfillment of followers' needs (Greenleaf, 1998). Leaders who are more concerned about others than themselves are humble, and their humility stimulates strong relationships with followers and encourages followers to become fully engaged in their work (Owens & Hekman, 2012). Liden, Wayne, Zhao, and Henderson (2008) identified seven dimensions of servant leadership (see bulleted list). As you look to grow, strengthen, and empower teacher leaders, we recommend you scheduling time with your emerging teacher leaders to have genuine conversations about the following:

- Emotional healing or sensitivity to personal setbacks of colleagues
- Creating value for the community, encouraging others to engage in volunteer activities
- Problem-solving skills
- Task knowledge that provides assistance to colleagues
- Empowering behaviors that help colleagues grow and succeed
- Putting colleagues first

- Ethical behavior

KEY TAKEAWAYS

The key takeaways are components that each administrator or aspiring teacher leader must understand to grow and develop teacher leaders in his or her building or district. Additionally, the section allows for readers to identify their own key takeaways from Phase 5. This is a way to reflect on your learning to grow teacher leadership or to develop as a teacher leader.

- During the Nurture phase most administrators individualized their role and increased their influence in nurturing their recruited teacher leaders.
- Many administrators discussed leadership in general and leadership styles in particular with their recruited teacher leaders.
- Teacher leaders during the Nurture phase need support and encouragement from their supervisors.

List Your Own Takeaways in the Space Provided

_____

_____

_____

_____

CHAPTER SUMMARY

The Nurture phase requires that school administrators work closely with each teacher leader and provide personalized coaching and mentoring. No matter how effective the teacher leader is, he or she will need the school administrator to counsel them. Keep in mind, Michael Jordan, arguably the best basketball player of all time, needed a coach to mentor him in his early years in the NBA. As coaches nurtured his skills, Jordan grew to be a better leader on the court and a better teammate. This example illustrates what should occur when nurturing teacher leaders. The school administrator, throughout the Nurture phase, assists the teacher leader to become a better teacher in the classroom and a better school leader.

We recommend that school administrators embrace the uniqueness of each teacher leader during this phase. Throughout the nurturing process, recognize (using whichever platform the school uses for such things) the accomplishments and achievements of teacher leaders. The most difficult facet during the Nurture phase might be how you encourage your teacher leaders when they experience setbacks and obstacles.

There is no way to predict when or how this will occur. Providing recognition to teacher leaders throughout the Nurture phase not only helps teacher leaders strengthen their self-confidence, but also helps to strengthen the school's support for teacher leadership. It is important that others hear about the positives of teacher leadership so that the culture of teacher leadership in your school is strengthened.

Nurturing teacher leaders must not be restricted to the normal constructs that often prevent the development of true leadership capacity. Based on our responses, we believe that many school administrators realize the importance of teacher leadership's ability to adapt over time to meet the needs of the school, students, and teachers. Adaptability is also important when it comes to nurturing teacher leaders. The components and strategies that are found in the nurturing phase for teacher leaders must be governed by school's culture, student achievement, and the complexities of the day that schools face.

SIX

Phase 6: Empower Teacher Leaders

My first administrative job was in a small K–8 school in southwestern Minnesota. The total student population was 127. Ironically, I graduated from the school (when it was still a K–12) 17 years before being hired. The school board was willing to take a chance on "one of their own" to run, and I mean run, the school. How much of a chance? I had yet to earn my administrative license so they hired a part-time superintendent to mentor me. He came once a month for school board meetings but aside from that, I was on my own.

Before taking this job, I had spent 11 years as a high school social studies teacher and head volleyball coach. I didn't know much about being an administrator let alone how to run a school, but they hired me and said they trusted me. I can still remember the school board chair (who happened to be my father's cousin) say, "Mike, you are hereby

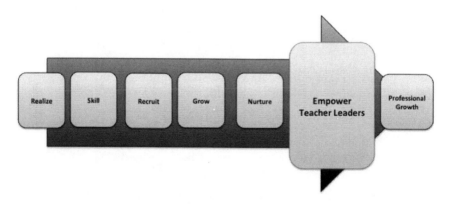

Figure 6.1.

empowered to make decisions that will make or break this fine school. Don't mess it up."

We tell this story to offer perspective, perspective about how we interpret the word *empower*. When you are empowered you are, to a degree, on your own. Much like the part-time superintendent, someone is there to ensure that things don't go awry. There is a fine line that the administrator needs to walk during this phase. Your teacher leaders need freedom during this phase but the skillful administrator knows how to oversee the process and intervene only when necessary. We mentioned a few different times before that in this phase the new recruit isn't new anymore. These teacher leaders have passed through the Growth and Nurture phases and are ready to take on some real responsibilities.

During the Growth and Nurture phases they have experienced what it is like to initiate or be a part of a project to fruition. It would have been easier, if in our research, we stated how we defined the word, but thought it would be interesting to see how our respondents rationalized their interpretations. We did the same, without coming right out and saying it, with Nurture in the previous phase. Any qualitative researcher worth his salt knows not to ask leading questions. We simply asked what empowerment meant to them and how they empower their teacher leaders in their schools.

The first place we go for teacher leader information (sometimes inspiration) is the Teacher Leader Model Standards (TLMS). Unfortunately, although mentioned many times, the word *empower* is not defined by the Teacher Leadership Exploratory Consortium. Many authors have offered their definition of empowerment as it relates to teacher leadership that is included in the table.

Taken all together, the research and definitions provide an excellent, albeit varied, definition of empowerment. Our research, as you will soon read, aligns best with that of Midgley and Wood (1993) and Acker-Hocevar and Touchton (1999) with the focus on team and being given the authority to make informed decisions. Trust, like many before, was affirmed by our research as well.

In the opening example, even though empowered, I can say with 100 percent certainty that I had no idea what I was doing, but I did figure it out after a time. If you have done your due diligence, your teacher leaders should have some semblance of understanding about what they need to do in their new positions. You, or you and your team, have groomed and prepared them for what is to come. The hardest part for you during this phase might be to stay out of their way and allow them to experience what it is like to be empowered and to make informed decisions without your direct input.

The opening example also speaks to the importance of empowerment without abandonment. In our experience and speaking to administrators, we have noticed that teacher leaders far too often are empowered and

Author(s), Date	Definition(s)
Acker-Hocevar & Touchton, 1999	Given power
Midgley & Wood, 1993	Shared decision making
DiRanna, Loucks, & Horsley, 2001	Bring about change
Katzenmeyer & Moller, 2001 Marks & Lewis, 1997	Opportunities to create personal knowledge/increase student learning
York-Barr & Duke, 2004	Contribute to school curriculum and policy
Crowther, Kaagan, Ferguson, & Hann, 2002 Bryk & Schneider, 2002 Hoy & Sweetland, 2001 Short, Greer & Michael, 1991 Hoy & Miskel, 2008	Trust
Childs-Bowen, Moller, & Scriven, 2000	Work with stakeholders
Hallinger & Richardson, 1988	Increase access to resources

then left to their own devices to figure things out. Though many teacher leaders ultimately do, we strongly encourage that empowerment doesn't equate to abandonment. One of our respondents stated, "I let my teachers fly. I explain my vision and ask if they can help make it a reality. I only set parameters if necessary."

Another commented, "By guiding them and allowing them to do some of the work and use their talents." Neither statement embodies empowerment as we see it. As we stated previously, there is a fine line between abandonment and trust. Too much freedom and not enough influence doesn't equate to empowerment.

Teacher leadership is too critical not to have a plan of empowerment that includes support. We believe administrative support is necessary to overcome any obstacles that may arise. It is important to remember that even the best leaders need varying levels of support from time to time and teacher leaders are no different. Support can come from you or a delegated mentor who understands what successful leadership looks like in your district. Teacher leaders during the Empowerment phase must have the ability to experience leadership and also the added support that is meant to help, not smother, their leadership development.

PULSE CHECK

- How often do you allow others the opportunity to make authentic decisions that affect or impact their grade level, school, or district?

If you answered to the contrary, what steps can be taken today to remedy this?

• What specific strategies do you use to empower others to be part of the decision-making process in your school?

RESEARCH QUESTIONS AND EXPLANATION OF FINDINGS

The research questions that guided our research during this phase were:

1. What does empowerment of teacher leaders mean?
2. How are teacher leaders empowered to be leaders in your school?

Obviously, the focus of these two research questions is on empowerment. Closer examination will reveal to the reader that in the first research question, empowerment is a noun where in the second research question, empowered is verb. This was done purposefully in our attempt to look at this phase from two different angles. The first question focuses on examples of liberation and authorization. The second question focused on examples of inspiration and encouragement. Taken together, we were hoping to discover examples of what administrators did to slowly diminish their influence and allow more freedom for their teacher leaders.

As you may recall, we mentioned the importance of inspiration and encouragement early in the recruitment phase—inspiring and encouraging teachers to become leaders. School administrators must inspire and encourage teacher leaders during this phase to step out of their zones of comfort, push the boundaries of their abilities, and be true school leaders in school. Furthermore, it is during this phase that teacher leaders help others aspire to also become leaders. As we contend, an inspiring school leader leads to inspired stakeholders who aspire to succeed and to be great.

Before moving on, we think it important to examine how we arrived at this phase by revisiting the Growth and Nurture phases before providing our definition of empowerment.

• *Growing teacher leaders is the process of allowing teacher leaders to develop and acquire the skills necessary to be successful.* Growing is all about presenting opportunities for your newly recruited teacher leaders, that is, a series of learning opportunities or single events that assist the teacher leader to understand leadership and their new role within the school.

• *Nurturing teacher leaders is the process of continued/ongoing mentorship and coaching by school administrators.* Nurturing is the continued support of school administrators to fine-tune the skills and strategies teacher leaders learned or acquired throughout the growth process. As stated in the (growing) definition, the trial-and-error period is over. At this juncture, your newly recruited teacher leaders should be showing promise.

- *Empowerment is achieved when the teacher leader has acquired the proper skills needed to make informed decisions (individually or as part of a group) that affect their school or district.* The hand-holding is over and the training wheels are off. A word that embraces this phase is *confidence.* The administrator is confident that the teacher leader will get the job done. Isn't this, after all, what teacher leadership is all about? Quite simply, it is shared leadership as opposed to the authoritative bureaucracy that plagues those districts that haven't embraced teacher leadership.

Research Questions: What does empowerment of teacher leaders mean, and how are teacher leaders empowered to be leaders in your school?

Each stage we have examined so far has been important. This stage is distinctive because it marks a point of departure away from the ordinary for administrators. Most administrators usually do something similar to what has been mentioned in Phases 1 to 5 in their regular duties. For example, in Chapter 2, we mentioned metacognition and the importance of being a reflective practitioner. In Chapter 4, we mentioned the administrator's job to create opportunities for teachers to develop and acquire skills to be successful. You don't need to be developing teacher leaders to perform these tasks.

As we explained, empowerment means letting go of some duty or responsibility and turning the reigns over to one of your teacher leader recruits. For those that have been in the dark regarding your efforts to build teacher leadership capacity, this might come as a shock. For example, during this phase a teacher leader will now be in charge of the Outreach Program, which was mentioned in Chapter 4 under Recommendations. The administrator will oversee the Outreach Program, but will no longer be directly in charge. Teachers, parents, and community members will now be working with the teacher leader, freeing the administrator up to attend to more pressing issues.

We hypothesized that the answers to our first research question might elicit responses contrary to our definition of empowerment. We were right and wrong. The responses did give us pause to wonder how many of our respondents had actual experience in this phase, and which did not. The responses also affirmed some of the results of research performed before ours. Many of our respondents characterized this phase by stating the role trust plays in empowerment. This finding was discerned by many researchers before us.

As we stated, trust was a common response to our question about empowerment. In answer to our first research question, one administrator stated, "Trusting staff to lead projects and various activities in the school; having high expectations of a leader within the school and being explicit about roles and responsibilities." Another asserted, "Providing a system and means for them to lead and make a difference, that they are reliable and a vital part of our success." Another suggested, "TRUST implicit in the senior leader's offer of opportunities and empowerment. This faith may very well provide impetus to those who don't recognize their own potential and ability."

Because the high number of responses to our research questions that were analogous to those found in Phases 4 and 5, we questioned whether some administrators had experienced moving through the Empowerment phase. Many responses muddled the lines between growth/nurture and our meaning of empowerment. Here are a few examples:

- "Freedom to try and freedom to learn from mistakes." *This is too similar to the Growth phase where opportunities and freedom are commonplace.*
- "Allow the person some decision-making opportunities." *The teacher leader in the Empowerment phase has almost unrestricted decision-making authority.*
- "Allow teachers to take risks and monitor instruction among their peers." *Once again, risk taking is a characteristic of the Growth phase.*
- "The opportunity to lead combined with the opportunity to make mistakes that do not impact unduly on students, the community or other colleagues." *Similar to Growth and Nurture phases.*
- "Allowing teachers to be able to have a go and make their own mistakes and successes and to have the ownership of the experience." *Comparable to the Nurture (mistakes) but reaches into the Empowerment with comment about ownership.*
- "Giving them opportunities so they can see their strengths." *Parallel to the Nurture phase where the teacher leader is given opportunities to analyzes their strengths but still not to the Empowerment phase. During the Empowerment phase, the teacher leaders would know their strengths and would be using them to the best of their abilities.*

We list these not to disparage our respondents, quite the contrary. We list them to emphasize the difference between Empowerment and the phases that preceded it. We have a full understanding of the difficulties school administrators face as they look to create collaborative leadership constructs, as we too have sat in the principal's chair. Respondents that clearly articulated empowerment as it relates to teacher leadership focused on ownership and responsibility. Unfortunately, those examples were few and far in between.

We see this as a breakthrough rather than as a shortcoming of our research. Our research verifies that even though it is often mentioned as beneficial, true collaborative leadership using teacher leaders is rarely established. The statements that follow either hit the mark, or come very near what we envision empowerment to look like in schools.

- "Providing opportunities to be part of school planning processes. Connecting teachers to leadership networks. Driving committees, projects and programs." *We believe this statement comes very near to the Empowerment phase. Our research methodology (survey) limits what we can reason what this administrator meant by (drive), but this verbiage indicates a step in the right direction.*

- "Teacher leaders are empowered to utilize resources in ways that they feel will improve student achievement. Teacher leaders play important roles in directing PLCs that focus on curriculum and instruction and data driven decision making." *We particularly like the idea that the teacher leaders can use resources as they see fit. The word* direct *seems to fit well with our definition of empower as well.*

- "My teacher leaders are put in charge of leading things, like teams, departments, taking active roles as members of the leadership team, lead major school projects, etc." *Taken together, the phrase* put in charge *and* lead major school projects *gets more to our vision of the Empowerment phase.*

- "The Principal delegates sections of the school plan as their responsibility and allows them the resources to be successful. The Principal then supports the teacher to ensure quality programs and practices are evident." *This statement captures the Empowerment phase nicely. Words like* responsibility, resources, *and* support *epitomize the Empowerment phase.*

Our results so far have concluded that very few of our respondents either reached the Empowerment phase or practiced the type of collaborative leadership that is necessary to grow teacher leaders. This doesn't mean that it never happens. Our outcomes could be a result of consequence. Quite possibly, many of our respondents never viewed teacher leadership as a situation in which they abdicate authority as completely as we insist. The reader should remember that in a true collaborative (or distributive) leadership structure, teacher leaders not only have a voice, or a seat at the decision-making table, but they are also given authentic responsibilities and duties.

You have done the work thus far and should be confident in their abilities. Those chosen have the characteristics (Phase 2), have agreed to journey down this leadership path (Phase 3), have been given opportunities to hone their leadership skills (Phase 4), and you have worked very closely with them to understand leadership and their leadership style (Phase 5). With these duties comes decision-making authority. As we stated previously, free from these tedious, although vital responsibilities, that are now being performed by teacher leaders, the administrator is now able to focus on more pressing obligations. Aside from reducing the administrative load, the most important benefit of the administrator will be an increase in time.

Time is a precious commodity for administrators in today's educational climate. With this extra time, the administrator might find, as we did, that they could be more present in the day-to-day operations of your school. More time equates to having an increased presence in the classrooms, in the hallways, and at important school functions. You might even get home to dinner at a decent hour.

Collaboration (in some way, shape, or form) was mentioned by enough of our respondents to be in this section as well. As you will soon read in our analysis on the importance of team, our respondents made clear the importance of not only them, but also other teacher leaders, collaborating during the Empowerment phase. One of our respondents asserted, "Personally, I gauge the level of effectiveness in this phase by focusing on the engagement of others and their ability to accomplish goals collaboratively."

Another administrator affirmed the importance of teacher leaders collaborating with each other by suggesting, "It's about embedding a collaborative professional learning culture that values the contributions and learning that everyone offers, values differentiated professional support, facilitates creative thinking and genuine opportunities for teacher leaders to make a difference."

Clearly, collaboration and creating opportunities for teacher leaders to talk to each other during this phase is important. York-Barr and Duke (2004) indicate that collaboration is often associated with effective forms of teacher leadership. We liken this situation to their first year as a teacher. Most school districts have a system in place where new teachers meet with each other periodically (monthly, in our experience).

At these monthly meetings new teachers have the opportunity to talk about their successes and challenges with others that are in the same boat. The administration normally has a focus for these meetings, district policies, classroom management, and the like. According to our research, your new teacher leaders should have some type of professional development strategy similar to what your new teachers have. It is the administrator's job to carve out time each month for the new teacher leaders to talk with one another.

The examination of collaboration segues nicely into our last focus area for the Empowerment phase. Honestly, this discovery took us by surprise and came as a result of looking over the comments that were associated with collaboration. Team, teaming, and teamwork were suggested time and time again by our respondents in answer to our two research questions. Team, as it relates to teacher leaders, was examined previously. What we discovered coincidentally was that many of our respondents were reporting about themselves and their desire to work collaboratively with their newly formed leadership groups. Some veterans of this new collaborative leadership construct spoke about how these teams already work together.

Those new to teacher leadership tended to make comments about their plans or aspirations for this newly formed leadership group. One administrator commented,

> We have a leadership team comprised of 4 teacher leaders, a counselor and myself. The leadership team is the pulse of the school and will make proposals, but we consistently survey teachers through the use of google forms because it is understood that consensus will move the group. Also, I am in the process of putting together an innovation team whose sole purpose will be to find ways to innovate and solve problems in different ways.

Another respondent reported similarly.

> Empowering teacher leader teams can mean several things. To me, it means that you truly work together as a team and realistically look at your organization and address the strengths and weaknesses together. The culture has been developed such that we can be transparent with each other, knowing we are all committed, support each other and we have structures in place to focus on the right work.

On the opposite spectrum, one of our more seasoned respondents commented,

> We spend time discussing the tough issues. I seek their advice when I have tough issues. We argue and debate the best course of action. We laugh together. Our professional development plans require a formal observation; however, due to the high levels of trust on our team, most of the feedback, planning and discussion happen. There is a departmental principle that observation is not in any way a method to judge performance. It's about building confidence and capacity around a specific set of skills.

Our experience has taught us how alienating and isolated administration can be at times. We both graduated with administrative degrees that focused on Educational Leadership, with an emphasis on leadership. We both became administrators because we wanted to focus on leadership. The reality is that very little of what current administrators do is directly related to leadership. School principals are often seen as both managers and leaders (Deal & Peterson, 1994; Duffie, 1991; Stronge, 1990, 1993).

School principals continue to struggle between the role of manager and leader (Jenkins, 2009). Dimmock (1999) provides one of the few distinctions among these concepts and also acknowledges that there are competing definitions.

> School leaders [experience] tensions between competing elements of leadership, management and administration. Irrespective of how these terms are defined, school leaders experience difficulty in deciding the

balance between higher order tasks designed to improve staff, student and school performance (leadership), routine maintenance of present operations (management) and lower order duties (administration). (p. 442)

To reiterate, our research indirectly suggests that one way current administrators can focus on leadership is by developing teacher leaders. Empowering teacher leaders strengthens the school principal's effectiveness in school, as well as, grows the leadership capacity in school, which is inherently needed in all schools. As Dimmock clearly explains, school administrators who grow and empower teacher leaders are considered to be leaders, and those school administrators who are reluctant to empower others are viewed as managers.

As schools face increasing complexities, they desperately need more school leaders, including teacher leaders. Leaders view the empowerment of others as a means to transform the school's culture, instructional processes, and long-term vision.

VIGNETTE

Mrs. Summer Macon is the principal of Wrightsville Middle School, a traditional middle school that over the past 3 years has experienced a change in student demographics. Wrightsville Middle School is located in the inner city of a growing metropolis. As a result, the middle school's demographics have changed dramatically. Many of the students come from single-parent households who are also transient. In addition, 20 percent of students come from homes where Spanish is the primary language.

Before the rapid change in demographics, the school enjoyed strong community support because many of the students who attended Wrightsville Middle School in the past were now small business owners or worked in white-collar jobs. The school enjoyed a strong parent volunteer program and community partnerships. Wrightsville Middle School consistently ranked among the top scoring middle schools in the state— never going without resources and supports because parents would always jumped in and volunteer, fund-raise, or donate supplies, equipment, and technology.

Since then, as the demographics changed, the support by parents and community partners has steadily declined. Parent volunteers are almost non-existent, and of the community partnerships that once existed, none of the partnerships are now active. Mrs. Macon continues to have the overwhelming support from parents and the faculty and staff because they all see her working long hours at school to the detriment of her health. She is always at school trying to make sure that the school provides the best learning environment for her students. Parents, the faculty and staff, and community members have noticed that she refers to the students at Wrightsville Middle School as her students.

Realizing that Mrs. Macon could not sustain her pace alone, a group of teachers, who are considered to be teacher leaders at Wrightsville Middle School, met with her after school. The teacher leaders took it upon themselves to schedule a time to meet with Mrs. Macon to try to figure out ways to help her and to help the teaching and learning process that was the best for students. The teacher leaders at Wrightsville Middle School, in large part, are grade-level leaders, authorized to make decisions, with limited oversight.

Mrs. Macon has given the teacher leaders the autonomy to make decisions necessary to make each of their grade levels work to the benefit of learning. As a result, they have been able to help the school maintain key learning components and programs, which have resulted in stable student learning. More specifically, Mrs. Macon places a great deal of emphasis on their role as leaders in the school.

The group of teacher leaders, with the approval of Mrs. Macon, decided to begin to take on more leadership roles in the school. Understanding the importance of community outreach programs in schools, the teacher leaders decided to take the lead on reestablishing many of the partnerships with the community that once existed and also to create new ones. They felt that Mrs. Macon should not shoulder the burden of forming partnerships alone because it should be a whole-school responsibility. Understanding that Mrs. Macon could not give more of her time to the school, they stepped up to the plate.

They created a leadership opportunity that will strengthen their school by identifying a need in the school. Furthermore, by their willingness to be leaders, they grow the capacity of the school to continue to offer the best learning program to students. Lastly, their leadership helps to extend the tenure of Mrs. Macon because she can reduce the amount of time she is at school.

PHASE 6 EMPOWERMENT RECOMMENDATIONS

We would hope that by this phase, the administrator can state with relative certainty that the teacher leaders you are currently working with have leadership aspirations, but not administrative aspirations. This, believe it or not, is not uncommon. Riggs (2013) surveyed teachers and found that nearly 25 percent of teachers were interested in a hybrid role of teaching and some sort of leadership position and that 84 percent of them were either "not very" or "not at all" interested in becoming a principal. He goes on to posit the following challenge, "Why does [leadership] have to mean a dean or a principal? We have to change our mindset about what school leadership is." In a very profound way, your efforts to grow and develop teacher leadership in your buildings are doing just that.

Individual Teacher Leader Meetings

The often frenetic and bureaucratized school settings that surround adults and young people limit opportunities for leaders to fully collaborate (Collay, 2004; Peterson, 1994). In light of Collay and Peterson's assertions, our recommendation is for you (or you and your team) to develop a year-long plan to have new teacher leaders meet with you individually (monthly) to discuss how things are going. We mentioned that new teacher leaders are similar to new teachers in some ways. The recommendation to meet frequently comes directly from our research for this phase that revealed the need for collaboration and team building. Just as it is beneficial for new teachers to discuss their successes and challenges, the same can be said for new teacher leaders.

The teacher leader's first year is truly experiential. We encourage administrators to insist that each teacher leader keep a weekly journal that details their experiences throughout the week. Experiential learning (and reflection using a journal) is grounded in David Kolb's Experiential Learning Theory (ELT; 1984). Kolb's ELT consists of four dimensions: concrete experience, reflective observation, abstract conceptualization, and active experimentation. These four dimensions are essential for the learner to gain knowledge, and ultimately, to learn from experience (Kolb, 1984).

Each time the new teacher leader and the administrator meet, we suggest the following tasks be addressed:

1. Sharing Session: the teacher leader will bring a minimum of one success and one challenge to be discussed at the meeting. What the teacher leaders have written in their journals should suffice.
2. School Vision: we feel strongly that it is important to keep the school's vision for teacher leadership at the forefront of each meeting. The administrator should reinforce the transformative nature of teacher leadership and how he sees this happening each week or month. It is important to cite specific examples from the works of current teacher leaders when doing so.
3. Current State/Plans for Future: each teacher leader should provide an update in regard to where he or she is in their efforts to advance and develop his or her function. The structure of this portion of the meeting should touch on previous work, current status, and future works that will be performed.

Transparency Check

This is probably not the best label for this section, but we think it will suffice. It is important to periodically enlighten the rest of the staff about what each of your teacher leaders have been doing when they are not in the classroom. This can be done in a variety of different ways. However you currently update your staff (newsletter, staff meeting, and weekly announcement) will do. The most important portion of your message is the focus on teaching and learning and what the teacher leaders are performing in these regards. Any suggestion or air of administrative connotations should be avoided at all cost.

KEY TAKEAWAYS

The key takeaways are components that each administrator or aspiring teacher leader must understand to grow and develop teacher leaders in his or her building or district. Additionally, the section allows for readers to identify their own key takeaways from Phase 6. This is a way to reflect on your learning to grow teacher leadership or to develop as a teacher leader.

- Empowerment is achieved when the teacher leader has acquired the proper skills needed to make informed decisions (individually or as part of a group) that affect their school or district.
- Empowerment, as it is related to teacher leadership, means many things to many different people. To us, empowerment means that the administrator is confident that the teacher leader will get the job done. The teacher leader is given authentic decision-making authority.
- Phase 6 is different from the previous phases for a variety of different reasons. Primarily, the administrator will *not* be performing certain duties that he or she might have done for several years.
- Not all administrators practice true collaborative leadership or adhere to empowering teacher leaders the way we encourage in this book.
- One way current administrators can focus on leadership is by developing teacher leaders.

List Your Own Takeaways in the Space Provided

_____

_____

_____

_____

CHAPTER SUMMARY

We realize that what we propose throughout this chapter (empowering teacher leaders) might seem a little peculiar, even for those familiar with *The Leader Within* or the TLMS. It might seem peculiar in the sense that we are pushing the envelope just a little. Our experience has taught us that if you allow certain teachers to have the freedom to explore, discover, research, and become inspired, great things can happen.

These teachers should be empowered to do more than what can be accomplished in their classrooms. We mentioned that the word *empower* is not mentioned in the TLMS and quite honestly, what we are proposing does push teacher leadership to the next level. For example, here are some definitions of what the standards maintain teacher leaders should be doing:

Domain 1 Function B: *Models* effective skills in listening, presenting ideas, leading discussions, clarifying, mediating, and identifying the needs of self and others in order to advance shared goals and professional learning

Domain 2 Function D: *Assists* colleagues in accessing and using research in order to select appropriate strategies to improve student learning

Domain 2 Function E: *Facilitates* the analysis of student learning data, collaborative interpretation of results, and application of findings to improve teaching and learning

We maintain that once you empower teacher leaders, they are in a position to make decisions for their grade level, school, or district. They have moved beyond modeling, assisting, and facilitating (although these activities guide what they do on a day-to-day basis when working with their colleagues) to creating something tangible. Some of the TLMS that elucidate what we are getting at are:

Domain 5 Function E: Collaborates with colleagues in the *design, implementation, scoring, and interpretation of student data* to improve educational practice and student learning

Domain 6 Function D: Collaborates with families, communities, and colleagues to *develop comprehensive strategies* to address the diverse educational needs of families and the community

Domain 7 Function D: Collaborates with colleagues to select appropriate opportunities to advocate for the rights and/or needs of students, *to secure additional resources* within the building or district that support student learning, and to communicate effectively with targeted audiences such as parents and community members

We began this chapter with a story so we thought it fitting that we end with a story as well. The origins of my journey to understand the complicated nature of teacher leadership began at a track meet years ago. I was talking with one of the track coaches about her duties at her school and she mentioned to me that she was put in charge of tracking (and making sense of) math data for three grade levels. Further inquiry revealed that she not only tracked data for this year, but for 3 prior as well. She went on to explain how she compiled the data by using state and national comprehensive math results as well as local (classroom data) results.

I could tell how proud she was of her work and was very impressed with how she described the trends she discovered that were occurring in two of the three grade levels. My next question was simply, "When are you going to talk to the teachers about this information?" What she said next shocked me. She told me that her principal was going to talk to the rest of the teachers about it at the next staff meeting. It seemed strange to me that the principal would share this information instead of her.

When I asked if she considered talking with her colleagues about what she had compiled her response was "I didn't think it was my place to talk to the rest of the teachers about this type of thing." I explained to her that she did the work, she compiled the data, she understood the trends better than anyone else, and that she should tell her principal that she wouldn't mind presenting this data to the rest of the staff at the next faculty meeting.

A few weeks later, I caught up with her and she told me that she was going to present her findings at the next staff meeting. She enthusiastically explained the title of her presentation (Math Data and Trends) and felt confident that her presentation was going to be well received by her colleagues. She went on to explain how her principal welcomed the idea and mentioned to her that he was a little relieved that she was willing to present because she was the expert, not him.

Fast forward 3 years and this very same coach received her master's degree with an emphasis in Teacher Leadership from the institution where I currently teach. Presently, she is still teaching and coaching track. In addition to this she has been put in charge of overseeing, tracking, and analyzing the math data and curriculum for her entire school.

The principal has allowed her to remain in her classroom, but she spends the last 2 hours of the day analyzing math data and curriculum. She meets with her principal once a month and presents her findings to her colleagues on a quarterly basis and presents to the school board twice a year. She is still known as Mrs. B to her students and Tammy to her colleagues. Although not given the formal title (Math Guru), everyone knows that she is a leader in her building and the go-to person if you have a question about math. She has become a true teacher leader.

SEVEN

Phase 7: Provide Ongoing Professional Growth Opportunities for Teacher Leaders

We both hope that you take some time (as we did when writing this chapter) to appreciate and reflect on your journey from the Realize phase to this last and final phase for growing teacher leaders. The first thing that might strike you as odd is that we did not call this phase "professional development or staff development." We believe that advancing the skills for teacher leaders is different from that of a teacher or administrator. We have experienced situations where, once an individual becomes a leader, a school principal, superintendent, or teacher leader, they fail to continue their growth.

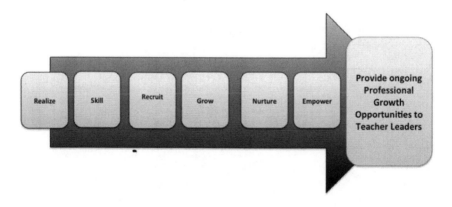

Figure 7.1.

As we contend in Chapter 6, this process of developing teacher leaders can be beneficial to administrators by allowing them to focus solely on leadership activities. Because of this difference we thought it fitting to call this phase Professional Growth Opportunities rather than professional development, which is often used for teachers and administrators.

Our involvement in PK–12 education has provided us with many professional development experiences as teachers and administrators. As administrators, we had the opportunity to plan and deliver professional development to our teachers and staff. We soon realized that professional growth for teacher leaders was different. Simply put, a teacher leader's particular skillset is unique from the competences needed by most administrators (which we were both very familiar with). For the final time we will reference the reader to Appendix B, which offers a comparison between administration and teacher leadership. Administrative tasks and duties are different from teacher leader duties. Providing growth opportunities for teacher leaders that are aligned to administrative competencies does not work.

In the same sense, providing teacher leaders with growth opportunities aligned to classroom teaching is also futile. Since the Growth phase you have been molding and transforming their talents for responsibilities outside of the classroom. Although most teacher leaders will still remain in their classrooms for a certain amount of time during the day, they were chosen to perform something quite different from their classroom duties. From our experience, it is often the best teachers who are recruited to be teacher leaders so they probably don't need much help in that area anyway.

As teachers are empowered to be leaders in our schools, it is important that school administrators instill in them the need for ongoing professional learning. As we mentioned in *The Leader Within*, teacher leaders are considered to be "lead learners" in school. Teacher leaders and school administrators must model the expectation to engage in effective and strategic professional learning. In the case of a teacher leader, they must engage in professional learning that will: strengthen their ability to lead, coach, or mentor; address a need in the school; and lead to growth as a teacher.

The words *professional growth opportunities* also attend to something that was referenced by Jim Knight and also something that was mentioned in the Recommendations Section from Chapter 6. Regarding traditional methods of professional development, Knight (2007) states,

> When one-shot professional development endeavors fail to take hold, teachers are often blamed for "resisting change." When in fact it's about *poorly designed professional development*. Teachers learn best when learning from each other, sharing lesson plans, assessments, activities, and ideas about individual students (p. 3).

In Chapter 6 we also recommended the development of an Individual Teacher Leader plan in which administrators meet individually, at least once monthly, with each of their new teacher leaders. It is important that the administrator focus on the word *opportunities* (plural) and not one opportunity. According to Supovitz and Christman (2005), school leaders must assist teachers in creating professional growth opportunities and experiences in the school, through collaborative learning communities.

This is also true for teacher leaders because professional growth must be embedded into daily practice. Zinn (1997) contends that most teacher leaders lack ongoing support which in turn creates barriers to their growth. Our hope is that the individual teacher leader meeting (ITL) with the administrator and also as a teacher leader group (TLG) will serve as that support.

To grow scale in the school, school leaders must assist teacher leaders in rethinking the traditional means of training to transform the school's culture and create a lasting change. Teacher leaders need highly effective professional growth opportunities that are more than just "canned" workshops. Instead, they need opportunities that push them to rethink their roles in school that will ultimately lead to improvements in student learning and leadership structures. Professional growth opportunities allows for teacher leaders to address the ongoing complexities that are found in schools by learning for capability and adaptability. What this plan might look like and what types of opportunities need to be provided is what this final chapter is all about.

Today's teacher leaders must devote a significant amount of time to professional growth. We feel that it is important to note the difference between professional learning and professional development. Based on our research and experience, professional development is considered to be a single learning event, whereas professional learning is considered to be an ongoing learning opportunity that happens over a period of time. Most educators view professional development as a 1-day training event. When they engage in professional growth opportunities, the learning occurs over a period of time. Furthermore, professional learning requires an evaluation of impact on growth. We firmly believe this can occur during the ITL and TLG sessions

From the beginning, we have stressed that schools are complex and dynamic organizations, even more so today. School administrators empower teachers to be leaders as a means to address and remove some of the many obstacles and barriers that prevent the school from moving forward. Professional learning and growth is at the core of transforming a culture and growing teacher leadership that is responsive to the needs of the school. Ultimately, to lead together, school administrators and teacher leaders must also engage in professional growth together. By learning together, school administrators and teacher leaders are better prepared to transform the school's culture focused on student learning through professional practice.

The reader should also realize that the format for this chapter is a bit different from the previous six chapters. Our research concluded with the Empowerment phase. We have done enough research to know that a dearth of literature addresses this important final phase. There is some literature that references professional development for teacher leaders and some that suggests teacher leaders manage professional development efforts in their school districts. The aim of this final chapter is to provide a collection of teachable skills that your teacher leaders can acquire and master through reflection (journaling) and experience.

PULSE CHECK

- What is the current state of your professional growth plan for your teacher leaders? How often do you or (your team of teacher leaders) meet?
- How do you provide your teacher leaders with professional growth opportunities that are embedded into daily practice and aligned to their professional growth?
- Do you engage in professional growth with your teacher leaders? How do you assist teacher leaders in their professional growth as school leaders?
- How are teacher leaders encouraged to engage in self-reflection before, during, and after professional growth opportunities?

PROFESSIONAL GROWTH PLAN FOR TEACHER LEADERS

As we stated previously, there are several teachable skills that teacher leaders must possess (as determined by previous research, our current research, and the Teacher Leader Model Standards [TLMS]). Our plan for the rest of this chapter is to provide a framework for the administrator to use to provide professional growth for your teacher leaders. Ash and Persall (2000) contend that principals must create an environment that supports collaboration among teachers; provides time for teacher's professional learning; and recognizes, rewards, and celebrates the concept of the teacher as leader. We couldn't agree more.

We will begin by analyzing the most important (in our humble opinions) skills and work our way down the list. It should be pointed out that each district is unique and where the administrator decides to start (and the order and pace in which to proceed) is indefinite. What we mean by this is if the greatest need in your district is to develop relationships between your school and the business community, then the administrator might want to begin with *Advocacy*. It should also be pointed out that administrators should meet with their teacher leaders twice a month. One meeting will be the ITL and the other will be the TLG meeting.

The TLG meetings are designed around a monthly schedule. Each month administrators will meet with all of their teacher leaders and reflect, share, learn, and plan around a new skill. We will present our information on a monthly schedule, but how administrators want to cover the material is totally up to them. For example, you might want to examine only 5 of the 10 skills and spend 2 months on each during the school year.

As we stated, it is totally up to you. There are certain elements that each TLG meeting needs to include. These elements were determined by taking bits and pieces from what has been examined in the book thus far. This TLG format is strictly for the administrator and how he or she wants to tailor the agenda that is shared with teacher leaders is flexible.

Finally, the configuration and pacing of these meetings serves an important purpose. The time between meetings allows the teacher leader to actually experience or practice the skill. This should allow for rich dialogue about each skill every time the TLG meets. Each teacher leader can discuss their unique experiences, and the other teacher leaders, it is hoped, will gain a better appreciation for the work their colleagues are performing.

First Meeting Only: Examination of Teacher Leader Skills

The administrator should provide teacher leaders with a brief overview of all of the skills and share the order in which these skills will be examined throughout the year. The order can also be determined by the group. The questions provided in each section should be used as a template or a format for the administrator to use. The amount of time needed for each section will be unique to each district and determined by the particular needs of the group (or individual) teacher leader.

It is not expected that each individual question will be examined or asked during the TLG. The purpose of the guiding questions is to begin professional dialogue not to serve as a lock-step process to proceed through each skill. The order in which we recommend you begin your examination is:

Communication
Organization
Adult Learning Theory
Listening and Collaboration
Facilitation
Reflection
Modeling
Big Picture

Advocacy and Presenting Ideas
Research

We recommend that each TLG meeting utilize the following format:

- *Report on progress made on previous month's skill.* Each teacher leader should share elements from their reflective journal to the rest of the group (See Reflective Journaling in Chapter 6). In our experiences, sharing experiences can be a powerful learning tool for all participants. Snell and Swanson (2000) affirm by stressing the importance of professional learning to help teacher leaders to cultivate expertise, collaboration, and reflective skills and a sense of empowerment.
- *Introduction and overview of new monthly Skill.* Here the administrator will discuss the new skill that will be examined.
- *Teaching the skill.* The administrator should provide some insight as to how this particular skill can be learned. As you will soon read, the TLG session itself is the perfect classroom and the administrator, the perfect teacher.
- *Activities that your teacher leaders can do to develop the skill.* This is often difficult to predict without knowing exactly what it is your teacher leaders are doing.
- *Possible venues to practice these skills.* This can and should act as a sharing session where the teacher leaders discuss possible settings for them to experience the skill firsthand.
- *Pulse check.* Similar to what we used in this book, this is a way for teacher leader to discuss their understanding of the skill and examine if this skill is considered a strength for them or a growth area.
- *Individual meeting schedule.* Aside from this meeting, each teacher leader will meet with the administrator at least once (the ITL meeting) before the next TLG meeting.
- *Introduction of next skill.* The administrator will announce the next skill that will be examined at the next TLG meeting.

As we indicated previously, the administrator can vary the order that the skills are addressed to meet the unique needs of their district. We do not recommend changing the elements that will be included in each TLG meeting. The amount of attention and time given to each skill is determined by the administrator. Next, we will begin our examination of the skills that will be discussed, analyzed, and taught during each TLG meeting.

COMMUNICATION

Introduction and Overview

You can introduce each section any way you wish. A good segue into each section is a brief journal sharing session where each teacher leader shares at least one meaningful experience from the previous month. How administrators want to use the journal is totally up to them. Our recommendation is to focus on these journal entries during the individual sessions, but they may be used in the manner described previously as well. If you need to create an overview of this skill, or any skill for that matter, reference each definition in the proceeding chapters.

In many cases, teacher leaders perform communication differently as they seek to use communication to engage diverse perspectives in the decision-making process. Teacher leaders often use one-on-one mentoring as the medium of choice to communicate to teachers, teacher leaders, and other stakeholders. Though teacher leaders use all available tools (such as social media and e-mail) to communicate, our research suggests that they overwhelmingly prefer face-to-face communication. Teacher leaders understand how relationships impact effective communication.

Questions and or Discussion

This section will provide hypothetical guiding questions that administrators can use to guide discussion about the particular skill. It should be pointed out that these questions are our recommendations and can be altered to meet the needs of each group, school, or district.

1. What is your preferred mode of communication?
2. What types of communication will you use in your current position?
3. How important is communication in your current position?
4. What are a few things you will need to do to develop this skill?

Teaching Communication

The way you are going to teach this and all the rest of the skills, for the most part, will occur during these TLG meetings. This will, in our estimation, be a welcome change for most administrators and a trip down memory lane as well. It might be helpful to prepare for each TLG meeting the same as you would when you used to teach, by developing a quality lesson plan.

This is a perfect opportunity for administrators to explain to the *teacher leaders* how they model quality communication in their current position. The administrator should have a variety of examples from e-mail, social media, newspaper articles, and staff, school, or district meetings. These examples should contain both written and verbal communication.

Our recommendation is to model communication by reviewing the steps you took in setting up this meeting, developing and sharing the agenda, and communication used during the meeting.

Questions and Discussion

1. What type of communication methods will you use primarily in your current position?
2. What are some of the most important elements your message should contain no matter what method of communication you are using?
3. How are you going to determine how successful your communication efforts were?

Activities or Possible Venues to Develop Communication as a Skill

As you will soon discover, it is difficult, if not impossible for us to come up with a broad list of activities that can be used to help all teacher leaders hone their communication skills. It really depends on what your teacher leaders are doing. For example, if one of your teacher leaders is put in charge of the Grades 3–6 Professional Learning Committee (PLC) efforts, these communication activities might include group e-mails, leading grade-level discussions, presenting information (via PowerPoint or Prezi) . . . take your pick. The important thing to determine is which communication efforts are currently being used, and more importantly, which forms of communication should be used?

Questions and Discussion

1. Is there a need to change or improve the method of communication that is currently being used in your current position? The answer to Question 3 might determine how this question is answered.
2. If the answer to the previous question was yes, what other activities can be performed that will enhance your communication efforts?
3. Do your current activities require more verbal or more written communication methods?
4. If it is determined that more verbal communication activities are needed, what are some future opportunities that would provide the teacher leader with the likelihood of evolving these skills? The same question can be discussed for written communication.

Pulse Check

This is an opportunity to see where the group is in regard to the particular skill being assessed. We think this is a good opportunity for all teacher leaders to appreciate and understand the work of the other teacher leaders and how they communicate to their constituents. Now is also a good time for the administrator to take notes for the individual conferences that will be held with each teacher leader in between TLG dates. Individual questions and insights can be addressed during these individual meetings to move the process forward.

1. Is there a need to go back and review any parts of the previous sections?

ITL and Next Skill

This is a time for administrators to schedule ITL meetings with their teacher leaders. It is also a good time to introduce the next skill (Organization) that will be introduced and provide ample time for the teacher leaders to form their own opinion about what the skill means to them. This is also a good time to remind the teacher leaders about their journaling exercises. They should be prepared to share with the group one meaningful experience at the beginning of the next session.

ORGANIZATION

Introduction and Overview

Organization is important for all leaders to understand to be effective in their role. Have your teacher leaders reflect on their current position and list the various organizational skills they need to employ to be effective. On any given day, the teacher leader might be coaching and mentoring teachers, advocating in the local community for additional supports and resources for students, as well as, facilitating professional learning communities.

According to Gehrke (1991) organizational skills help teachers to (1) continue teaching and improving one's own teaching; (2) monitor and evaluate current practice in the school; (3) coach and mentor others in developing effective curriculum and instructional practices; (4) engage in the decision-making process; (5) facilite and lead professional learning for others; and (6) create a culture of collaboration.

Questions and Discussion

1. What current training are teacher leaders currently provided in the area of organization?
2. How important is organization to teacher leaders? To leaders in general?
3. How does the organization of a teacher leader impact the teaching and learning process in schools?

4. How do the organizational skills needed for your new position compare to those employed in the classroom?

Teaching Organization

This is a perfect opportunity for administrators to explain to the teacher leaders how they model quality organizational skills in their current position. There should be plenty of authentic organizational skills that administrators needed to embrace when preparing for this session alone. We also recommend that administrators begin linking the skills as they proceed forward. For example, apart from organizational skills, mention the communication skills needed to prepare for this session as well. Our hope is that the teacher leader will discover that any action performed by leaders entails many skills, not just one particular skill. Organization is extremely difficult to teach, which is why modeling organization is the best way to teach teacher leaders how to be an organized leader.

Questions and Discussion

1. What actions can the teacher leaders perform that will demonstrate their organizational skills?
2. How can you develop the time-management skills that are needed to be successful?
3. What organizational skills are needed to be effective in your current position?

Activities or Possible Venues to Develop Organization as a Skill

We mentioned previously organizational skills are extremely difficult to teach, but not impossible. Why must teacher leaders be organized? It is our belief, through our experience as school administrators, that effective leaders must be organized. Being organized helps the teacher leader remain focused on the job at hand and on the ultimate goal of helping students to achieve. Leaders who are seen as unorganized jeopardize not only their ability to lead but also the success of the organization.

Questions and Discussion

1. Rate your organizational skills on a scale from 1 to 10 (10 being the ultimate organizational score). What can you do today to improve your score?
2. What other elements play an integral part to being organized (e.g., time management, goal setting, prioritization, self-awareness, focus, communication)?
3. Think about a time, in your role as a teacher leader, when you weren't as organized as you could have been. What were the

causes? What steps can you take now to ensure it doesn't happen again?

Pulse Check

1. Is there a need to go back and review any parts of the previous sections?

Individual Session and Next Skill

This is a time for administrators to schedule the individual meetings with their teacher leaders. It is also a good time to introduce the next skill that will be discussed (*Adult Learning Theory*) and provides ample time for the teacher leaders to form their own opinion about what the skill means to them.

ADULT LEARNING THEORY

Introduction and Overview

One of the epiphanies new administrators have when they move out of the classroom and into the principalship is that working with adults is a lot different than working with students. We both would agree that it is a little harder to do for a variety of reasons. Higher up on the rung of adult interactions is teaching adults. Teaching adults is definitely different than teaching students and even dissimilar to working with them. All teacher leaders will have worked with their colleagues before, so working with them now shouldn't be much different, or will it? We would like the reader to recall some of what was written in Chapter 4 about teachers and leadership. Barth (2013) warns of trying to make changes in a leveling profession.

> Teachers are, in a way, their own worst enemy when it comes to unlocking leadership because they don't welcome it, typically don't respect it, and often feel threatened by one of their own taking it on. Anyone who bumps above the level is subject to condemnation: "Who the heck do you think you are?!" I'm not talking about trends—I'm talking about people impeding teacher leadership. Some of the people are called principals, and some are called teachers. (p. 10)

If your teacher leaders are not aware of what Barth warns about in the previous section, we think this is a good place to begin your discussion about adult learning theory.

Questions and Discussion

1. On first blush, Barth's comments may seem cynical, but we have witnessed firsthand this very thing happening. Have your teacher leaders deliberate their assertions about teachers impeding teacher leaders and determine if this is an issue at your school.
2. How have your colleagues reacted to your new position? Are they interested in what you are doing?
3. Do your teacher leaders understand the major differences between teacher leadership and administration?

Teaching Adult Learning Theory

Andragogy (adult learning) is a theory that holds a set of assumptions about how adults learn. It uses approaches to learning that are problem based and collaborative rather than didactic (traditional lecturing or teacher "knows" model) and also recognizes more equality between the teacher and learner. Here are some tips when teaching about adult learning:

- Adults are autonomous and self-directed.
- Adults need to be free to direct their own learning.
- Adults bring knowledge and experience to each learning activity.
- Linking new material to learners' existing knowledge and experience creates a powerful and relevant learning experience.
- Adults need learning to be relevant and practical.
- Adults are problem-oriented and want to apply what they've learned.

Another resource that may prove to be valuable is Knight's (2007) *Instructional Coaching*, specifically, Chapter 3. The main focus of this chapter is what Knight calls the partnership philosophy. Although the partnership philosophy was intentionally written for instructional coaches, we believe it pertains to any situation where adults are working with other adults. According to the partnership philosophy, instructional coaches "see themselves as equal, respect others' choices, and encourage others to voice opinions" (p. 40).

The partnership philosophy is designed to build a trusting relationship between the instructional coach and the teacher with whom they are working. The partnership philosophy is built on the core principles of equality, choice, voice, dialogue, reflection, praxis, and reciprocity.

Equality: Instructional coaches and teachers are equal partners

- Teachers' ideas must count. "Equality does not mean that coaches and teachers have equal knowledge on every topic, but it does mean that the collaborating teacher's opinions are as important as the coach's and both points of view are worth hearing" (Knight, 2007, p. 41).

Choice: Teachers should have choice regarding what and how they learn

- Offering choices does not mean that everything is up for grabs. "Teachers have to strive to help their students meet standards, and if teachers are to be treated professionally, they must act professionally" (Knight, 2007, p. 43).

Voice: Professional learning should empower and respect the voices of teachers

- Coaches often learn the most when they carefully listen to the viewpoints of people who may appear to be disagreeing or resisting ideas being shared.
- "The coach needs to communicate that the other person's life is important and meaningful. This may be the most important service that a coach can provide" (Knight, 2007, p. 43). "Part of 'voice' is simply taking the time to truly hear what people have to say" (Knight, 2007, p. 44).

Dialogue: Professional learning should enable authentic dialogue

- "If people come together as equals, if they feel free to voice their opinions, if they are listened to, and if they act on the exhilarating belief that they are free to agree, disagree, and reflect on ideas as they choose, something marvelous can happen" (Knight, 2007, p. 46).

Reflection: Reflection is an integral part of professional learning

- "Reflective thinkers, by definition, have to be free to choose or reject ideas, or else they simply are not thinkers at all" (Knight, 2007, p. 47).
- According to Schon (1987), "reflection is necessary for learning since often the most important parts of skillful or artistic activities, like teaching, are hidden from our conscious understanding. People are skilled or artistic practitioners because they have a repertoire of competencies and skills that they may not even be able to identify" (p. 48).
- Reflection ultimately provides opportunities for teachers to think about what Parker Palmer (1998) calls "the inner landscape of the teaching self" (p. 48).

Praxis: Teachers should apply their learning to their real-life practice as they are learning

- When we learn, reflect, an act, we are engaged in praxis. "Praxis is *not* memorizing a new routine so that we can teach it in our classes exactly as we memorized it. True praxis is established when teachers have a chance to explore, prod, stretch, and recreate whatever they are studying" (Knight, 2007, p. 49).
- "Because reflection is central to this approach to learning, praxis enacted between people is impossible without a partnership relationship" (Knight, 2007, p. 50).

Reciprocity: Instructional coaches should expect to get as much as they give

- "[Instructional coaches] who operate from the partnership principles enter relationships with teachers believing that the knowledge and expertise of teachers is as important as the knowledge and expertise of the coach" (Knight, 2007, p. 50).

Activities or Possible Venues to Develop an Understanding of Adult Learning Theory

Honestly, this might be the easiest skill to develop because your teacher leaders will be interacting with their colleagues each and every day. We firmly believe that above all else, adults want to be respected. You might want your teacher leaders to focus on the six bulleted statements about adult learners and have them reflect on how they considered each when preparing for their next interaction with their colleagues.

This reflection can be written in their journal and shared at the next ITL meeting. The partnership philosophy is detailed and probably too cumbersome to examine in one sitting. It might be wise to have your teacher leaders' rate the importance of each of the eight elements (or) identify those that are used most often in their current position.

Questions and Discussion

1. Do you consider the elements of the Adult Learning Theory when you last communicated with the adults you are working with?
2. Share authentic instances where one or two (or more) of the elements of the partnership philosophy were evident in a conversation you have had with a colleague. It is possible that these elements were present but were not intentional.

Pulse Check, ILT, and Next Skill

This is a time for administrators to schedule the individual meetings with their teacher leaders. It is also a good time to introduce the next skill that will be discussed (*Listening/Collaboration*) and provides ample time for the teacher learners to form their own opinion about what the skill means to them.

LISTENING AND COLLABORATION

Introduction and Overview

All leaders must be effective communicators. Successful communication requires superior listening skills. One can't happen without the other. Teacher leaders are empowered to coach, mentor, and lead, all of which requires that the teacher leader be accessible to others and available to listen, gathering input and feedback, to engage others in transforming the school culture. Furthermore, listening invites diverse perspectives into the school's decision-making process. To sustain teacher leadership, conversations are crucial, which require a certain level of respectful listening (Lambert, 2002).

In our opinion, teacher leadership also helps to create a culture of collaboration. Teacher leadership and collaboration are interconnected, in other words, inseparable because both strengthen the other. Harris and Muijs (2003) describe the unique relationship between collaboration and teacher leadership, "Collaboration is at the heart of teacher leadership, as it is premised upon change that is enacted collectively" (p. 40). We must not forget that teacher leadership is focused on improving student achievement by creating a culture that is based on collaboration.

Question and Discussion

1. Discuss how you are provided opportunities to engage in collaboration in your current position.

Teaching Listening and Collaboration

It is important to realize and understand that, like with all forms of leadership, teacher leadership development is best done through authentic experiences. School administrators must provide their teacher leaders with opportunities to engage in leadership experiences where they can develop and continue to grow the skills needed to effectively listen and engage, lead or facilitate, in collaboration with others.

We would hope that this has already occurred during the Growth and Nurture phases. According to Hargreaves (1991), growing a culture of collaboration is essential to effective school leadership, including teacher leadership. There is no better way to hone leadership skills than by constant practice, engaging in rich leadership experiences, and learning through trial and error.

Questions and Discussion

Before moving on, we would also like to remind the reader what was written in the Adult Learning Theory section, specifically in regard to Knight's partnership philosophy. Two elements directly related to listening and collaboration are voice and dialogue.

1. How are you given opportunities to develop listening skills through rich, real experiences?
2. Is Knight's voice and dialogue a part of what you do in your collaborative efforts in your current position?
3. How often are you given opportunities to lead through collaboration?
4. How can collaborative leadership skills be developed internally?

Activities or Possible Venues to Develop Listening and Collaboration as Skills

The development and continued growth of listening and collaboration skills will vary from school-to-school and district-to-district. According to the TLMS, there are three different groups the teacher leader will collaborate with in their position. These are, in hierarchical order, colleagues, families, and administration.

Questions and Discussion

1. In your current position, which of the three groups will you need to collaborate with most often? Least often?
2. What different means of collaboration will you be using to collaborate with your constituents?
3. Reflect on your school setting, how are teacher leaders encouraged to engage in professional growth that targets listening and collaboration?
4. How is listening and collaboration identified as a skill that needs further development in teacher leaders?
5. How do school administrators assist teacher leaders in developing and growing leadership and collaboration skills?

Pulse Check, ILT, and Next Skill

This is a time for administrators to schedule the individual meetings with their teacher leaders. It is also a good time to introduce the next skill that will be discussed (*Facilitation*) and provides ample time for the teacher leaders to form their own opinion about what the skill means to them. This is also a time to remind the teacher leaders about their journaling exercises.

FACILITATION

Introduction and Overview

In our experience, teacher leaders will not need to use this skill as often as those mentioned previously, but often enough to merit a place somewhere in the middle of the pack. It is also our contention that many who need to organize and run a meeting have no background knowledge about how to do it correctly. A good facilitator is concerned with the outcome of the meeting or planning session, with how the people in the meeting participate and interact, and also with the process.

Although achieving the goals and outcomes that everyone wants are of course important, a facilitator also wants to make sure that the process is sound, that everyone is engaged, and that the experience is the best it can be for the participants. Once again, this is the perfect teachable moment for administrators to specify how they facilitate these TLG meetings.

Questions and Discussion

1. How often do you need to act as a facilitator in your current position?
2. Think about an instance where the facilitator did, in your estimation, a fantastic job. What were some of the things he or she did to make the presentation so engaging?
3. Think about one that didn't go so smoothly. What were some of the things that could have been done better?

Teaching Facilitation

As we have stated numerous times before, administrators should be teaching these skills during each of the TLG sessions. If you haven't already been doing so, we also think it is a good time to cover all of the previous skills that are being used during this session. Take a moment to touch on Communication, Organization, Adult Learning Theory, and Listening/Communication and discuss how each is being applied in this current session. Our contribution to this are the Question and Discussion sections, which were each developed with the ALT in mind.

To teach facilitation as a skill, the following essentials should be addressed. The Question and Discussion section for the analysis of teaching facilitation should involve a detailed conversation (possibly the development of a checklist) around the following facilitation skill concepts. It can be as simple as answering, "how does he or she make this happen?" after reading each item. Quality facilitators attend to each of these each time they organize a meeting:

1. Makes sure everyone feels comfortable participating.
2. Develops a structure that allows for everyone's ideas to be heard.
3. Makes members feel good about their contribution to the meeting.
4. Makes sure the group feels that the ideas and decisions are theirs, not just the leader or presenters.
5. Supports everyone's ideas and does not criticize anyone for what they've said.
6. Is neutral and never takes sides.

Activities or Possible Venues to Develop Facilitation as a Skill

We hope, and are fairly certain, that by this time, all teacher leaders have had some experience with facilitation. Quite possibly, as early as the Growth phase, the teacher leaders were given the opportunity to be a part of a group that needed to present their ideas in front of their peers. In the Nurture phase, maybe they presented by themselves at a faculty meeting or in-service day. It is the administrators' responsibility to determine how often they believe teacher leaders will need this particular skill in their current position.

A tremendous activity for your teacher leaders to perform has to do with something that was mentioned in Chapter 6. We called it Transparency Check. Have your teacher leaders practice their facilitation skills by presenting at the next staff meeting. Each would be responsible for explaining to the rest of the staff what they are currently doing. We recommend that the planning and preparation for this meeting be done outside of the TLG and with as little oversight by the administrator as possible. Instead of discussing journal notes at the next TLG meeting, the teacher leaders should rehash how they sensed the meeting went and which of the six items were successful and which still need work.

Question and Discussion

1. Which of the six items from Teaching section went well and which did not go as well? Are there possible solutions for those that need attention?

Pulse Check, ILT, and Next Skill

This is a time for administrators to schedule the individual meetings with their teacher leaders. It is also a good time to introduce the next skill that will be discussed (*Reflection*) and provides ample time for the teacher leaders to form their own opinion about what the skill means to them.

REFLECTION

Introduction and Overview

We would hope that what we had written toward the end of Chapter 6 in regard to the reflective journaling exercise each teacher leader is currently doing would suffice for this segment. Each teacher leader should have the routine of sharing their reflections during both the ITL and TLG sessions. To carry the conversation and analysis to a higher level, we turn to John Dewey. In 1933, Dewey described the difference between impulsive action, routine action, and reflective action. The first, Dewey suggested was based on trial and error. The second relied on more traditional ways of operating, often times indorsed by authority.

However, Dewey claimed that reflective action arose from the work of educators who were active, who persistently and carefully considered how they practiced and what they were teaching, and was often the result of a need to solve a particular problem. Dewey (1933) suggests, "Reflective thought is a chain (which) involves not simply a sequence of ideas but a consequence" (p. 4).

Question and Discussion

1. What does the quote from Dewey mean to you and how can it be applied to your current position?

Teaching Reflection and Activities or Venues to Practice Reflection

We believe that it is best to analyze these next two segments during the ITL sessions. Having an open dialogue about personal thoughts, opinions, and aspirations might be too intimate for some to have in a public setting. We think that at this point, most teacher leaders are probably at either the impulsive or routine action stage described. Ideally, the teacher leader would progress to the reflective action stage, but to do so, the following questions should be considered and discussed with each teacher leader during the ILT sessions. How administrators want to examine and discuss each question is totally up to them. We think that the teacher leader (or anyone for that matter) becomes more proficient in the art of reflection by considering how the following pertains to them.

Questions and Discussion

Observation: How observant are you in regard to observing the behavior of others, and observing how others respond to your behaviors?

- How important is modeling appropriate behavior in your current position?

Reasoning: How sensible or logical are you (or have you been in the past) in regard to educational topics, initiatives, programs that directly affected you and your work here at the school?

- How do you respond to someone who is not thinking logically (too subjective) about a particular topic?

Responsibility: Your new role as a teacher leader has thrusted many new responsibilities upon you. How do you think you have managed these new responsibilities?

- How comfortable have you been acting independently and making decisions without direct oversight?

Open Mindedness: How receptive are you (or have you been in the past) to the views and knowledge of others?

- How have you, in your current position, allowed others to express their views and recognized these views even though they might run contrary to your own? (*Reflecting on facilitation might initiate a good conversation*).

Pulse Check, ILT, and Next Skill

This is a time for administrators to schedule the individual meetings with their teacher leaders. It is also a good time to introduce the next skill that will be discussed (*Modeling*) and provides ample time for the teacher leaders to form their own opinion about what the skill means to them.

MODELING

Introduction and Overview

Modeling describes the process of learning or acquiring new information, skills, or behavior through observation, rather than through direct experience or trial-and-error efforts. Learning occurs as a function of observation, rather than direct experience. We discussed at length the ranking or status modeling deserved and thought about placing it higher on our list. As you will see in the Activities or Venue section, modeling entails many of the skills that are listed in this chapter.

This is yet another opportunity for the administrator to (model) this important skill. To this point, the administrator has modeled appropriate communication, organization, adult learning, listening, facilitation, and reflection skills. Modeling is directly related to demonstrating or exhibiting the proper sequence or procedure. Many teacher leaders have used, and continue to use, modeling in their classrooms when teaching certain topics. Showing students how to do something is a powerful teaching strategy but, as you will soon read, is also a skill needed by teacher leaders in a variety of different areas.

Question and Discussion

1. In your current position, what are some things that might need to be modeled for your constituents?

Teaching Modeling

It might be easiest to model facilitation skills simply because it was the skill that was analyzed in the previous session. The administrator can choose to model any skill they wish. Just like in the classroom, the administrator will need to determine which parts of the skill need to be or can be modeled. For example, here are the six items that were listed in our analysis of Facilitation Skills. In educational terms, these are the objectives. We italicized those that can be modeled.

1. Makes sure everyone feels comfortable participating.
2. Develops a *structure that allows for everyone's ideas to be heard*.
3. Makes members feel good about their contribution to the meeting.
4. Makes sure the group feels that the *ideas and decisions are theirs, not just the leader/presenters*.
5. *Supports everyone's ideas and not criticizing* anyone for what they've said.
6. Is *neutral and never takes sides*.

Activities or Venues to Practice Modeling

An authentic activity for teacher leaders might involve their observing administrators' facilitation of an upcoming meeting. Administrators can model appropriate facilitation (well, any skill discussed up to this point for that matter) and have the teacher leaders rate their (facilitation) performance based on the six criteria listed previously. Administrators can choose to discuss the teacher leaders' analysis in place of the journal sharing that normally initiates each TLG meeting.

Because it is impossible to define the venues that teacher leaders might use to practice modeling as a skill, we will turn to the TLMS to provide the activities where teacher leaders may find themselves modeling.

Domain 1/Function B: Models effective skills in listening, presenting ideas, leading discussions, clarifying, mediating, and identifying the needs of self and others in order to advance shared goals and professional learning.

Domain 2: The teacher leader understands how research creates new knowledge, informs policies and practices and improves teaching and learning. The teacher leader models and facilitates the use of systematic inquiry as a critical component of teachers' ongoing learning and development.

Domain 4: The teacher leader demonstrates a deep understanding of the teaching and learning processes and uses this knowledge to advance the professional skills of colleagues by being a continuous learner and modeling reflective practice based on student results. The teacher leader works collaboratively with colleagues to ensure instructional practices are aligned to a shared vision, mission, and goals.

Domain 6/Function B: Models and teaches effective communication and collaboration skills with families and other stakeholders focused on attaining equitable achievement for students of all backgrounds and circumstances

Another good activity would be to have teacher leaders look over the Domains/Functions and identify which associated skills they would need to comprehend and grasp in addition to modeling.

Pulse Check, ILT, and Next Skill

This is a time for administrators to schedule the individual meetings with their teacher leaders. It is also a good time to introduce the next skill that will be discussed (*Big Picture*) and provides ample time for the teacher leaders to form their own opinion about what the skill means to them.

BIG PICTURE

Introduction and Overview

Our recommendation for this skill is that it be dealt with during the individual sessions with teacher leaders. As the teacher leader hones his/ her leadership skills, it is extremely important that the teacher leader is able to appreciate how his or her role is connected to the overall school's vision.

Teacher leadership at the surface is about empowering an individual to become a leader. However, as teacher leaders get into the role and continue to develop into a school leader, they garner a better understanding and recognition that teacher leadership is about creating structures and a school culture that supports the school's vision and student success. To be clear, as we have said repeatedly, teacher leadership must be strategically empowered and aligned to the school's vision. The vision for teacher leadership and school vision must work in unison to transform the school from one that is plagued by silos to one that is characterized by a laser focus on student success through collaborative leadership structures.

Teacher leaders, like all great leaders, realize that the positon is much bigger than the individual who holds the position. They understand that their success is determined by their effectiveness in serving and empowering others and growing a culture that is conducive to shared, distributed, and collaborative leadership. Teacher leaders see the big picture past their position and role, to exactly how they can help others and assist in leading school transformation. Too often, leaders are only leaders in title, but fail to accept the awesome responsibility that the position brings with it. Many fall victim to the position. To be successful, teacher leaders must remain focused on the work, the big picture of ensuring that students succeed.

Question and Discussion

1. Discuss how you are trained on making decisions based on the big picture? How often does your school administration model and discuss with you, one-on-one, the need to make decisions based on the school's vision.

Teaching the Big Picture

The best way to teach teacher leaders how to look at the big picture is to actually immerse them in making decisions. With training teacher leaders with understanding the big picture, embedded, individualized professional growth opportunities will be the ideal way because of the help teacher leaders gain an understanding of the size and responsibility of the position. Nevertheless, we must not forget that the school's organization plays heavily into "big picture" thinking. According to Leithwood and Jantzi (2010) teacher leaders, like educational leaders, are impacted by the elements of the school organization. Teacher leaders must be provided learning opportunities that will help the teacher leader understand the big picture and also help them develop the skills to work through the organization to succeed.

Questions and Discussion

1. How are you provided opportunities that will assist you in understanding the school's culture and organization?
2. How often are you given opportunities to discuss the big picture
   with others?
3. Discuss how you collaborate with others to understand the
   school's vision.
4. Does your school have a clear, measurable school vision and vision
   for teacher leadership?
5. If so, discuss. If not, how does teacher leadership help connect the
   dots (the big picture) in your school?

Activities or Possible Venues to Develop the Big Picture as a Skill

Big-picture thinking is obviously big for the school as an organization,
the school's culture, and more importantly, student learning. Everything
must work together, as seamlessly as possible, so that the focus of the
work remains on student success. Big-picture professional growth must
be embedded into the daily work of the teacher leader. Big-picture understanding will not occur without truly understanding the school's organization. It will be important that the school administrator work closely
with teacher leaders to continue their growth of understanding the big
picture.

Questions and Discussion

1. Reflect on your school setting, how are teacher leaders encouraged
   to engage in professional growth that targets understanding the
   big picture?
2. How is big-picture thinking and leading identified as a skill that
   needs further development in teacher leaders?
3. How do school administrators assist you in developing and growing leadership skills that will help you lead more effectively
   through big picture thinking?

Pulse Check, ILT, and Next Skill

This is a time for administrators to schedule the individual meetings
with their teacher leaders. It is also a good time to introduce the next skill
that will be discussed (*Advocacy and Presenting Ideas*) and provides ample
time for the teacher leaders to form their own opinion about what the
skill means to them.

ADVOCACY AND PRESENTING IDEAS

Introduction and Overview

We believe that these two skills are quite similar. In the interest of space, we thought we would combine the two. Our primary focus will be on advocacy, but the way we see it, you can't advocate for something without also presenting your ideas. In the interest of uniformity, we would like administrators to model this for their teacher leaders by presenting (in however much detail as they would like) how they advocated for building a culture for teacher leadership back in the Realize or Recognize phases. This conversation can be as thorough (many details and handouts, calendars, research) or vague as desired.

Cuthbertson (2014) states, "Seeing ourselves as teacher-leaders and advocates for public education is key. If we don't see ourselves in this role, we leave the door open for others outside the profession to tell our stories and determine the successes (and shortcomings) of our schools." Advocating can be as simple as a one on one conversation with a parent or as detailed as preparing public comments and testifying before a local school board, state board of education, or other governing body.

Questions and Discussion

1. Discuss with the group what you remembered about the meeting where you learned about the opportunity to become a teacher leader.
2. What were some of the questions you had following the presentation? Did you know where to find the answers?
3. Briefly explain to the group an experience you have had where you advocated for something.

Teaching Advocacy

Teacher leaders not only understand the processes needed to properly advocate for the needs of students, but they also understand how to obtain resources to support teaching and learning. The following five stages can be a helpful guide for teacher leaders to use when trying to secure additional resources.

1. Define objectives. What is it exactly that the group is advocating for?
2. Gather evidence to build an argument. What is it exactly that is needed?
3. Understand others' interests and resources. Are there other groups or individuals in the district with similar needs? Are there other

groups or individuals that might have the resources you are seeking?

4. Present a clear case. Make certain the group you are presenting to understands exactly what you are advocating for and that the topic has been thoroughly investigated. If your group is presenting to the school board, be prepared to answer questions about cost, cross-curricular or multigrade applications, and demonstrate how what you are advocating for aligns with the district's vision and mission. If your group is presenting to a group of parents, understand that it is difficult for them to be objective. Focus on how it is going to support their child.

5. Amend your proposal based on the feedback obtained—be prepared for this contingency. A teacher leader prepares for this possibility and has Plan B already in the works.

Questions and Discussion

1. Which of the previous five steps are you familiar with and exercised in your previous efforts to advocate? Which are you unfamiliar with?

2. Do you see yourself performing this process in your current position? How so?

3. How will you go about discovering other groups with similar needs?

Activities or Possible Venues to Develop Advocacy as a Skill

Some of these were listed under the Introduction and Overview. It is almost impossible to list possible settings without actually knowing what function or role the teacher leader currently has. We are relatively certain that all teacher leaders will need to advocate (present ideas) in some fashion during their tenure. Domain 3 Function F in the TLMS states, the teacher leader advocates for sufficient preparation, time, and support for colleagues to work in teams to engage in job-embedded professional learning. A possible activity might involve discussing how to advocate for the two underlined items.

Question and Discussion

1. Can you think of specific items or issues that you will need to advocate for in your current position?

Pulse Check, ILT, and Next Skill

This is a time for administrators to schedule the individual meetings with their teacher leaders. It is also a good time to introduce the next skill that will be discussed (*Research*) and provides ample time for the teacher leaders to form their own opinion about what the skill means to them.

RESEARCH

Introduction and Overview

In our experience, the most common type of research that is performed in the K–12 setting is action research. Ash and Persall (2000) define action research as the "implementation of innovative practices coupled with an assessment of those practices on student learning" (p. 15). Richard Sagor (2000) asserts,

> Practitioners who engage in action research inevitably find it to be an empowering experience. Action research has this positive effect for many reasons. Obviously, the most important is that action research is always relevant to the participants. Relevance is guaranteed because the focus of each research project is determined by the researchers, who are also the primary consumers of the findings. (p. 3)

Sagor has also outlined a seven-step process for performing action research in the educational setting.

1. *Select a focus.* Why does it merit further investigation?
2. *Clarify theories.* What values, beliefs, and theoretical perspectives do researchers hold relating to your focus? This is similar to performing a short literature review. Select at least three sources.
3. *Identify research questions.* Select one or two research questions.
4. *Collect data.* It is important here to use multiple sources of classroom data.
5. *Analyze data.* Answer the following questions: (1) what does the data say and (2) what is your interpretation of the data?
6. *Report results.* This can be done informally with your colleagues (at lunch, during a PLC) or formally (with administration).
7. *Take informed action.* Explain how your research will inform your teaching.

Questions and Discussion

1. How familiar are your teacher leaders with the action research process described?
2. Has there been a need to perform action research recently?

Teaching Action Research

The teaching portion of this session involves an examination of each of the seven steps outlined previously. The best possible scenario is if something (a new teaching strategy or initiative, for example, one-on-one technology) had recently been implemented at your district. Quite possibly, one of the teacher leaders was a member of the committee that researched and proposed the initiative. They can share their experiences with the rest of the group. Whether real or hypothetical, it is imperative that all members of the TLC have a firm grasp of each of the seven steps.

Questions and Discussion

1. Have one (or more) of your teacher leaders share their experiences performing action research. Quite possibly, the administrator will need to share their research experiences. Some teacher leaders might need to share what they performed as a part of their graduate coursework to earn their master's degree.
2. Is there a possibility that you will need to perform research in your current position?
3. How comfortable are you in leading a research effort?
4. Which of the seven stages are you least comfortable with?

Activities or Possible Venues to Develop Action Research as a Skill

It may or may not be safe to state that all of your teacher leaders are venturing into the unknown, so to speak. Each has become comfortable teaching in their classroom where the state designates particular standards and benchmarks that must be taught and expectantly learned by the students. The leadership skills they need to enhance as teacher leaders are different from those employed in the classroom. The decisions they make in their new positions will affect more than just their students in their classrooms, but possibly an entire grade level or more. Also, they are not always going to be told what to do or how to proceed. This independence, the thrill of the unknown is what drove us both toward administration. We have learned through experience that taking any initiative through the seven stages will safeguard the leader from being accused of hurriedly making decisions. Taking new initiatives through the seven stages will substantiate for most, that the decision to support the initiative was done with the best interest of all in mind.

Questions and Discussion

1. Are there any initiatives you have observed in your new position that might need to be taken through the seven stages of the action research process?
2. If you are currently planning on implementing a new initiative, have you followed the seven steps? Where are you in your planning? Is it too late to go back and reconsider your actions using the seven steps as a guide?

Final Thoughts on Growing Teachers Within

Throughout both *The Leader Within* and *Growing Leaders Within*, we continually stressed that growing teacher leaders is not a destination, but a journey. Growing leaders is not an easy process, in fact, many attempt to grow leaders only to fail as a result of (1) not having a vision for teacher leadership, (2) not having a well-developed plan, (3) not understanding teacher leadership, and (4) not having the capacity to grow teacher leaders. Many schools have good intentions as they begin to grow and develop some of their teachers into leaders, but ultimately fail to connect the dots. According to Day, Zaccaro, and Halpin (2004), little attention is given to describing or explaining the leadership growth process. In the case of teacher leadership, we suppose this might be because the absence of literature devoted to a true growth process for teacher leaders. Chapter 7 is our remedy to this deficiency.

In *Growing Leaders Within*, we offered a research-based seven phase growth process that is supported by our experience, numerous conversations with colleagues, and now our research. As noted by Avolio and Gardner (2005), developing leaders involves complex processes. Additionally, Kesler (2002) explains that developing leaders is a difficult process to measure, but it can be successful with a clearly defined process. In the interest of austerity, we developed a simple growth process that includes an appraisal (Our Recommendations) at the end of each step. We were hoping that the acronym RRRGNEP would end up representing an actual word, but no luck.

Step 1: Realize Teacher Leadership Is Essential.
Step 2: Recognize Teacher Leadership as a Teachable Skill.
Step 3: Recruit Teachers to become Teacher Leaders.
Step 4: Grow Leadership Capacities Among Teachers.
Step 5: Nurture Leadership Qualities in Teachers.
Step 6: Empower Teacher Leaders.
Step 7: Provide Ongoing Professional Growth Opportunities to Teacher Leaders.

As we close this chapter of our teacher leadership journey, we can't help ourselves but look at what the future might entail. We wanted to write a book about teacher leadership, check . . . *The Leader Within*. We wanted to research the subject of teacher leadership and develop a pragmatic process that could be used in almost any progressive district that embraced collaborative leadership and nurturing teacher leaders, check . . . *Growing Leaders Within.*

Our next foray will perhaps have something to do with the development of Professional Learning Networks explicitly for teacher leaders. Maybe, it will feature Teacher Leader Best Practices that highlight the skills mentioned in Chapter 7, and then some. The possibilities are endless. Take care.

Michael and Brian

Appendix A

Each survey had the same information preceding the survey questions.

Dear Principal/Superintendent/Administrator:

You are invited to participate in a study of your perceptions and experiences related to the growth and development of teacher leaders in your school/district. Our hope is that your responses will better inform us in our efforts to establish a process of growing teacher leadership. You were selected as a possible participant in this study because you have been identified as someone who is currently working with and nurturing teacher leaders. If you decide to participate, please complete the open-ended questionnaire that follows. Your submission of this questionnaire is implied consent. The questionnaire is designed to gather information from each of the seven phases of what we believe is essential to the selection, development, and empowerment of teacher leaders. In addition to this, questions about the continuous improvement of teacher leaders are included. It will take between 10 and 15 minutes to complete the questionnaire. No benefits accrue to you for answering the questionnaire, but your responses will be used to help us understand what is already being done in schools to promote and foster teacher leadership. Any discomfort or inconvenience to you derives only from the amount of time taken to complete the questionnaire. You may be asked to participate in a follow-up interview. These interviews will be either face to face or over the phone. Please indicate your willingness in the section below by answering yes or no.

Any information that is obtained in connection with this study and that can be identified with you will remain confidential and will not be disclosed. We will do our best to keep your personal information confidential. You may use a pseudonym if desired. To help protect your confidentiality: (1) storage of data and notes will be kept in a secured location accessible only to the research team; (2) purging of all personally identifiable information from transcripts and research reports submitted to us. If we write an article or book about this research project, your identity will be protected to the fullest extent possible. This research project may involve making digital audio recordings of your interview conversations. The digital audio recordings, accompanying notes, and transcriptions will be kept on a password-protected computer. Information from this study will be kept until September 2017 when all information will be destroyed. If you decide to participate, you are free to discontinue or refuse the follow-up interview at any time.

Please feel free to ask questions regarding this study. You may contact either researcher if you have additional questions. Contact Dr. Mike Coquyt, School of Teaching and Learning, Lommen Hall 216C, 218-477-2019, michael.coquyt@mnstate.edu or Dr. Brian Creasman 606-748-8303, bcreasman@cu-portland.edu. Any questions about your rights may be directed to Dr. Lisa I. Karch, Chair of the MSUM Institutional Review Board at 218-477-2699 or by e-mail at: irb@mnstate.edu.

Thank you for your time.

Sincerely,
Dr. Mike Coquyt & Dr. Brian Creasman

Survey #1

1. What was it (epiphany, moment) that made you realize the need for teacher leadership in your school?

_____

_____

_____

2. What are the essential skills that teacher leaders must have to be effective leaders?

_____

_____

_____

3. How is the importance of teacher leadership communicated to stakeholders?

_____

_____

_____

4. How do you allow for experimentation and learning, followed by repeated practice for your teacher leaders?

_____

_____

_____

5. How are teachers provided opportunities to learn and develop skills needed to be school leaders?

_____

_____

_____

6. What does empowerment of teacher leaders mean?

_____

_____

_____

Survey #2
1. Why are teacher leaders needed (critical) in your school?

_____

_____

_____

2. What are the key characteristics you look for in a prospective teacher leader?

_____

_____

_____

3. How are teachers encouraged to become teacher leaders?

_____

_____

_____

4. What types of meaningful learning challenges have you created for your teacher leaders?

_____

_____

_____

5. How do school administrators nurture teacher leaders throughout the growth process?

_____

_____

_____

6. How are teacher leaders purposefully empowered to be leaders in your school?

_____

_____

_____

Survey #3
1. How are teacher leaders essential to the school's long-term success?

_____

_____

_____

2. How are the essential leadership skills acquired or learned by teacher leaders?

_____

_____

_____

3. What are the major components of your recruitment plan for teacher leaders?

_____

_____

_____

4. What is the role of school administrators in the development of teacher leaders?

_____

_____

_____

5. What does the coaching and mentoring of teacher leaders look like?

_____

_____

_____

6. How do you go about evaluating your teacher leaders' work (observing the leaders' work with colleagues)?

_____

_____

_____

Appendix B

Effective School Characteristic No. 1: Clear and shared focus

Everybody knows where they are going and why. The focus is on achieving a shared vision, and all understand their role in achieving the vision. The focus and vision are developed from common beliefs and values, creating a consistent direction for all involved.

The Role of an Education Leader	The Role of a Teacher Leader
An education leader develops the capacity for distributed leadership *(ISLLC 2011 3d)*	*A teacher leader* utilizes group processes to help colleagues work collaboratively to solve problems, make decisions, manage conflict, and promote meaningful change *(TLMS 1a)*
	A teacher leader serves as a team leader to harness the skills, expertise, and knowledge of colleagues to address curricular expectations and student learning needs *(TLMS 4d)*
An education leader monitors and evaluates the impact of the instructional program *(ISLLC 2011 2i)*	*A teacher leader* facilitates the collection, analysis, and use of classroom—and school-based data to identify opportunities to improve curriculum, instruction, assessment, school organization, and school culture *(TLMS 4a)*
An education leader promotes the use of the most effective and appropriate technologies to support teaching and learning *(ISLLC 2011 2h)*	*A teacher leader* uses knowledge of existing and emerging technologies to guide colleagues in helping students skillfully and appropriately navigate the universe of knowledge available on the Internet, use social media to promote collaborative learning, and connect with people and resources around the globe *(TLMS 4e)*

Effective School Characteristic No. 2 : High standards and expectations for all students

Teachers and staff believe that all students can learn and meet high standards. Although recognizing that some students must overcome significant barriers, these obstacles are not seen as insurmountable. Students are offered an ambitious and rigorous course of study.

The Role of An Education Leader	The Role of a Teacher Leader
An education leader collects and analyzes data and information pertinent to the educational environment *(ISLLC 2011 4a)*	*A teacher leader* assists colleagues in accessing and using research in order to select appropriate strategies to improve student learning *(TLMS 2a)*
An education leader monitors and evaluates progress and revises plans *(ISLLC 2011 1e)*	*A teacher leader* facilitates the analysis of student learning data, collaborative interpretation of results, and application of findings to improve teaching and learning *(TLMS 2b)*
An education leader builds and sustains productive relationships with community partners *(ISLLC 2011 4d)*	*A teacher leader* uses knowledge and understanding of different backgrounds, ethnicities, cultures, and languages in the school community to promote effective interactions among colleagues, families, and the larger community *(TLMS 6a)*
An education leader collects and uses data to identify goals, assess organization effectiveness, and promotes organizational learning *(ISLLC 2011 1b)*	*A teacher leader* teaches and supports colleagues to collect, analyze, and communicate data from their classrooms to improve teaching and learning *(TLMS 2d)*

Effective School Characteristic No. 3: Effective school leadership

Effective instructional and administrative leadership is required to implement change processes. Effective leaders are proactive and seek help that is needed. They also nurture an instructional program and school culture conducive to learning and professional growth. Effective leaders can have different styles and roles—teachers and other staff, including those in the district office, often have a leadership role.

The Role of an Education Leader	The Role of a Teacher Leader
An education leader collaboratively develops and implements a shared vision and mission *(ISLLC 2011 1a)*	*A teacher leader* collaborates with colleagues and school administrators to plan professional learning that is team-based, job-embedded over time, aligned with content standards, and linked to school/district improvement goals *(TLMS 3a)*
An education leader obtains, allocates, aligns, and efficiently utilizes human, fiscal, and technological resources *(ISLLC 2011 3b)*	*A teacher leader* uses information about adult learning to respond to the diverse learning needs of colleagues by identifying, promoting, and facilitating varied and differentiated professional learning *(TLMS 3b)*
An education leader promotes the use of the most effective and appropriate technologies to support teaching and learning *(ISLLC 2011 2h)*	*A teacher leader* identifies and uses appropriate technologies to promote collaborative and differentiated professional learning *(TLMS 3d)*
An education leader maximizes time spent on quality instruction *(ISLLC 2011 2g)*	*A teacher leader* advocates for sufficient preparation, time, and support for colleagues to work in teams to engage in job-embedded professional learning *(TLMS 3f)*

Effective School Characteristic No. 4: High levels of collaboration and communication

There is strong teamwork among teachers across all grades and with other staff. Everybody is involved and connected to each other, including parents and members of the community, to identify problems and work on solutions.

The Role of an Education Leader

An education leader develops the instructional and leadership capacity of staff *(ISLLC 2011 2f)*

An education leader collects and uses data to identify goals, assess organization effectiveness, and promotes organizational learning *(ISLLC 2011 1b)*

An education leader ensures teacher and organizational time is focused to support quality instruction and student learning *(ISLLC 2011 3e)* .

An education leader promotes understanding, appreciation, and use of the community's diverse cultural, social, and intellectual resources *(ISLLC 2011 4b)*

The Role of a Teacher Leader

A teacher leader collaborates with colleagues and school administrators to plan professional learning that is team-based, job-embedded, sustained over time, aligned with content standards, and linked to school/district improvement goals *(TLMS 3a)*

A teacher leader works with colleagues to collect, analyze, and disseminate data related to the quality of professional learning and its effect on teaching and student learning *(TLMS 3e)*

A teacher leader engages in reflective dialogue with colleagues based on observation of instruction, student work, and assessment data and helps make connections to research-based effective practices *(TLMS 4b)*

A teacher leader uses knowledge and understanding of different backgrounds, ethnicities, cultures, and languages in the school community to promote effective interactions among colleagues, families, and the larger community *(TLMS 6a)*

Effective School Characteristic No. 5: Curriculum, instruction, and assessments aligned with state standards

The planned and actual curricula aligned with the essential academic learning requirements. Research-based teaching strategies and materials are used. Staff understands the role of classroom and state assessments, what the assessments measure, and how student work is evaluated.

The Role of an Education Leader	The Role of a Teacher Leader
An education leader collects and analyzes data and information pertinent to the educational environment *(ISLLC 2011 4a)*	*A teacher leader* assists colleagues in accessing and using research in order to select appropriate strategies to improve student learning *(TLMS 2a)*
An education leader monitors and evaluates the management and operational systems *(ISLLC 2011 3a*	*A teacher leader* facilitates the analysis of student learning data, collaborative interpretation of results, and application of findings to improve teaching and learning *(TLMS 2b)*
An education leader builds and sustains productive relationships with community partners *(ISLLC 2011 4d)*	*A teacher leader* supports colleagues in collaborating with the higher education institutions and other organizations engaged in researching critical educational issues *(TLMS 2c)*
An education leader promotes continuous and sustainable improvement *(ISLLC 2011 1d)*	*A teacher leader* collaborates with colleagues in the design, implementation, scoring, and interpretation of student data to improve educational practice and student learning *(TLMS 5b)*

Effective School Characteristic No. 6: Frequent monitoring of learning and teaching

Effective instructional and administrative leadership is required to implement change processes. Effective leaders are proactive and seek help that is needed. They also nurture an instructional program and school culture conducive to learning and professional growth. Effective leaders can have different styles and roles—teachers and other staff, including those in the district office, often have a leadership role.

The Role of an Education Leader

The Role of a Teacher Leader

An education leader maximizes time spent on quality instruction *(ISLLC 2011 2g)*

A teacher leader advocates for sufficient preparation, time, and support for colleagues to work in teams to engage in job-embedded professional learning *(TLMS 3f)*

An educational leader creates a comprehensive, rigorous, and coherent curricular program *(ISLLC 2011 2b)*

A teacher leader engages in reflective dialogue with colleagues based on observation of instruction, student work, and assessment data and helps make connections to research-based effective practices *(TLMS 4b)*

An education leader develops assessment and accountability systems to monitor student progress *(ISLLC 2011 2e)* *An education leader* ensures a system of accountability for every student's academic and social success *(ISLLC 2011 5a*

A teacher leader collaborates with colleagues in the design, implementation, scoring, and interpretation of student data to improve educational practice and student learning *(TLMS 5b)*

Effective School Characteristic No. 7: Focused professional development

A strong emphasis is placed on training staff in areas of most need. Feedback from learning and teaching focuses extensive and ongoing professional development. The support is also aligned with the school or district vision and objectives

The Role of an Education Leader	The Role of a Teacher Leader
An education leader creates and implements plans to achieve goals *(ISLLC 2011 1c)*	*A teacher leader* utilizes group processes to help colleagues work collaboratively to solve problems, make decisions, manage conflict, and promote meaningful change *(TLMS 1a)*
An education leader collects and analyzes data and information pertinent to the educational environment *(ISLLC 2011 4a)*	*A teacher leader* assists colleagues in accessing and using research in order to select appropriate strategies to improve student learning *(TLMS 2a)*
	A teacher leader facilitates the analysis of student learning data, collaborative interpretation of results, and application of findings to improve teaching and learning *(TLMS 2b)*
An education leader creates a personalized and motivating learning environment for students *(ISLLC 2011 2c*	*A teacher leader* serves as a team leader to harness the skills, expertise, and knowledge of colleagues to address curricular expectations and student learning needs *(TLMS 4d)*

Effective School Characteristic No. 8: Supportive learning environment

The school has a safe, civil, healthy and intellectually stimulating learning environment. Students feel respected and connected with the staff and are engaged in learning. Instruction is personalized and small learning environments increase student contact with teachers.

The Role of an Education Leader	The Role of a Teacher Leader
An education leader safeguards the values of democracy, equity, and diversity *(ISLLC 2011 5c)*	*A teacher leader* facilitates colleagues' self-examination of their understandings of community culture and diversity and how they can develop culturally responsive strategies to enrich the educational experiences of students and achieve high levels of learning for all students *(TLMS 6c)*
An education leader builds and sustains positive relationships with families and caregivers *(ISLLC 2011 4c)*	*A teacher leader* develops a shared understanding among colleagues of the diverse educational needs of families and the community *(TLMS 6d)* *A teacher leader* collaborates with families, communities, and colleagues to develop comprehensive strategies to address the diverse educational needs of families and the community *(TLMS 6e)*
An education leader considers and evaluates the potential moral and legal consequences of decision making *(ISLLC 2011 5d)* *An education leader* promotes social justice and ensures that individual student needs inform all aspects of schooling *(ISLLC 2011 5e)*	*A teacher leader* collaborates with colleagues to select appropriate opportunities to advocate for the rights and/or needs of students, to secure additional resources within the building or district that support student learning, and to communicate effectively with targeted audiences such as parents and community members *(TLMS 7c)*

Effective School Characteristic No. 9: High level of family and community involvement

There is a sense that all have a responsibility to educate students, not just the teachers and staff in schools. Families, as well as businesses, social service agencies, and community colleges/universities all play a vital role in this effort.

The Role of an Education Leader	The Role of a Teacher Leader
An education leader builds and sustains productive relationships with community partners *(ISLLC 2011 4d)*	*A teacher leader* uses knowledge and understanding of the different backgrounds, ethnicities, cultures, and languages in the school community to promote effective interactions among colleagues, families, and the larger community *(TLMS 6a)*
An education leader promotes understanding, appreciation, and use of the community's diverse cultural, social, and intellectual resources *(ISLLC 2011 4b)*	*A teacher leader* models and teaches effective communication and collaboration skills with families and other stakeholders focused on attaining equitable achievement for students of all backgrounds and circumstances (TLMS 6b)
An education leader safeguards the values of democracy, equity, and diversity *(ISLLC 2011 5c)*	*A teacher leader* facilitates colleagues' self-examination of their own understandings of community culture and diversity and how they can develop culturally responsive strategies to enrich the educational experiences of students and achieve high levels of learning for all students *(TLMS 6c)*

Bibliography

PREFACE

Crowther, F., Kaagan, S., Ferguson, M., and Hann, L. (2009). *Developing teacher leaders: How teacher leadership enhances school success.* Thousand Oaks, CA: Corwin Press.

Levin, B., and Schrum, L. (2017). *Every teacher a leader: Developing the needed dispositions, knowledge, and skills for teacher leadership.* Thousand Oaks, CA: Corwin Press.

CHAPTER 1

Barth, R. (2001). Teacher Leader. *Phi Delta Kappa,* 443–449.

Boyd-Dimock, V., & McGree, K. M. (1995). Leading change from the classroom: Teachers as leaders. Issues . . . about Change, 4(4). Retrieved from: http://www.sedl.org/change/issues/issues44.html

Creasman, B., & Coquyt, M. (2016). *The leader within: Understanding and empowering teacher leaders.* Lanham, MD: Rowman & Littlefield.

Fullan, M. (2005). *Leadership and sustainability: System thinkers in action.* Thousand Oaks, CA: Corwin Press.

Harris, A., & Muijs, D. (2002). Teacher leadership: A review of research [Electronic Version]. *University of Warwick.* Retrieved 1/22/2017 from http://forms.ncsl.org.uk/mediastore/image2/randd-teacher-leadership-full.pdf

Hatcher, R. (2005). The distribution of leadership and power in schools. *British Journal of Sociology of Education, 26*(2), 253–267.

CHAPTER 2

Allio, R. (2005). Leadership development: Teaching versus learning. *Management Decision, 43*(7/8), 1071–1077.

Ash, R., & Persall M. (2000). The principal as chief learning officer: Developing teacher leaders. *NASSP Bulletin, 84*(616), 15–22.

Badarocco, J. L., Jr. (2002). *Leading quietly: An unorthodox guide to doing the right thing.* Boston, MA: Harvard Business School Press.

Barth, R. (2001). Teacher Leader. *Phi Delta Kappa,* 443–449.

Creasman, B., & Coquyt, M. (2016). *The leader within: Understanding and empowering teacher leaders.* Lanham, MD: Rowman & Littlefield

Collins, J. (2001). Level 5 leadership. *Harvard Business Review,* January.

Crowther, F., Kaagan, S., Ferguson, M., & Hann, L. (2009). *Developing teacher leaders: How teacher leadership enhances school success.* Thousand Oaks, CA: Corwin Press.

Cuthbertson, J. (2014). How to become a teacher advocate. *Education Week Teacher.* Retrieved February 11, 2016, from http://www.edweek.org/tm/articles/2014/11/25/ctq-cuthbertson-teacher-advocate.html

Doh, J. (2003). Can leadership be taught? Perspectives from management educators. *The Academy of Learning Management and Education, 2,* 54–67.

Flavell, J. H. (1979). Metacognition and cognitive monitoring: A new area of cognitive-developmental inquiry. *American Psychologist, 34*, 906–911.

Flavell, J. H. (1987). Speculations about the nature and development of metacognition. In F. E. Weinert & R. H. Kluwe (Eds.), *Metacognition, motivation, and understanding* (pp. 21–29). Hillside, NJ: Lawrence Erlbaum Associates.

Greenleaf, R. K. (1998). *The power of servant-leadership.* San Francisco, CA: Berrett-Koehler.

Holland, C. J., & Kobasigawa, A. (1980). Observational learning: Bandura. *Theories of learning: A comparative approach,* 370–403.

Knight, J. (2007). *Instructional coaching.* Thousand Oaks, CA: Corwin Press.

Kouzes, J., & Posner. B. (2002). *The leadership challenge.* San Francisco, CA: Jossey-Bass.

Leithwood, K., Day, C., Sammons, P., Harris, A., & Hopkins, D. (2006). *Successful school leadership: What it is and how it influences pupil learning.* London, UK: DfES. Available at http://www.dfes.gov.uk/research/data/uploadfiles/RR800.pdf

Moller, G., & Pankaka, A. (2013): *Lead with me: A principal's guide to teacher leadership.* New York, NY: Routledge.

Rosenholtz, S. (1989). *Teachers' workplace: The social organization of schools.* New York, NY: Longmans.

Sagor, R. (2000). *Guiding school improvement with action research.* Alexandria, VA: ASCD.

Schon, D. (1987). *Educating the reflective practitioner.* San Francisco, CA: Jossey-Bass.

Schraw, G., & Dennison, R. S. (1994). Assessing metacognitive awareness. Contemporary Educational Psychology, 19 , 460–475.

Strodl, P. (1992). A model of teacher leadership. Paper presented at the Annual Meeting of the Eastern Educational Research Association.

Wilson, M. (1993). The search for teacher leaders. *Educational Leadership, 50*(6), 24–27.

York-Barr, J., & Duke, K. (2004). What do we know about teacher leadership? Findings of two decades of scholarship. *Review of Educational Research, 74*(3), 255–316.

CHAPTER 3

Ackerman, R., & Mackenzie, S. (2006). Uncovering teacher leadership. *Educational Leadership, 63*(8), 66–70.

Barth, R. (1991). Restructuring schools: Some questions for teachers and principals. *Phi Delta Kappan, 73*(2), 123–128.

Creasman, B., & Coquyt, M. (2016). *The leader within: Understanding and empowering teacher leaders.* Lanham, MD: Rowman & Littlefield.

Crowther, F., Kaagan, S., Ferguson, M., & Hann, L. (2002). *Developing teacher leaders: How teacher leadership enhances school success.* Thousand Oaks, CA: Corwin Press.

Donaldson, G. (2006). *Cultivating leadership in schools: Connecting people, purpose, and practice* New York, NY: Teachers College Press.

DuFour, R., & Eaker, R. (1998). *Professional learning communities at work: Best practices for enhancing student achievement.* Bloomington IN: National Education Service.

Katzenmeyer, M., & Moller, G. (2001). *Awakening the sleeping giant: Helping teachers develop as leaders.* Thousand Oaks, CA: Corwin Press.

Wynne, J. (2001). Teachers as leaders in education reform [Electronic Version]. *Eric Digest* from http://www.ericdigests.org/2002-4/teachers.html

CHAPTER 4

Allio, R. (2005). Leadership development: Teaching versus learning. *Management Decision, 43*(7/8), 1071–1077.

Barth, R. (2001). Teacher Leader. *Phi Delta Kappa,* 443–449.

Barth, R. S. (2013). The time is ripe (again). *Educational Leadership, 71*(2). Retrieved from http://www.ascd.org/publications/educational-leadership/oct13/vol71/ num02/The-Time-Is-Ripe-%28Again%29.aspx

Bierly, C., Doyle, B., & Smith, A. (2016). Transforming schools: How distributed leadership can create more high-performing schools. Retrieved from http://www.bain.com/Images/BAIN_REPORT_Transforming_schools.pdf

Bolman L., & Deal T. (2006). *Reframing organizations: Artistry, choice, and leadership.* San Francisco, CA: Jossey-Bass

Donaldson, G. (2006). *Cultivating leadership in schools: Connecting people, purpose, and practice.* New York, NY: Teachers College Press.

Gurvis, J., McCauley, C., & Swofford, M. (2016). *Putting experience at the center of talent management* [White Paper]. Retrieved from Center for Creative Leadership: https://www.ccl.org/wp-content/uploads/2016/07/TalentManagement.e-1.pdf

Searby, L., & Shaddix, L. (2008). Growing teacher leadership in a culture of excellence. *Professional Educator, 32*(1), 1–9

CHAPTER 5

Devaney, K. (1987). *The lead teacher: Ways to begin.* New York, NY: Carnegie Forum on Education and the Economy.

Greenleaf, R. K. (1998). *The power of servant-leadership.* San Francisco, CA: Berrett-Koehler.

Hart, A. (1990). Impacts of the school social unit on teacher authority during work redesign. *American Educational Research Journal, 27*(3), 503–532.

Liden, R. C., Wayne, S. J., Zhao, H., & Henderson, D. (2008). Servant leadership: Development of a multidimensional measure and multi-level assessment. *The Leadership Quarterly, 19*(2), 161–177.

Lieberman, A., Saxl, E. R., & Miles, M. B. (1988). Teacher leadership: Ideology and practice. In A. Lieberman (Ed.), *Building a professional culture in schools* (pp. 148–166). New York, NY: Teachers College Press.

Owens, B., & Heckman, D. (2012) Modeling how to grow: An inductive examination of humble leader behaviors, contingencies, and outcomes. *Academy of Management Journal, 55*(4), 787–818.

Wasley, P. (1989). Lead teachers and teachers who lead: Reform rhetoric and real practice. Paper presented at the annual meeting of the American Educational Research Association, San Francisco, CA.

CHAPTER 6

Acker-Hocevar, M., & Touchton, D. (1999, April). A model of power of social relationships: Teacher leaders describe the phenomena of effective agency in practice. Paper presented at the meeting of the American Educational Research Association, Montreal, Canada.

Collay, M. (2004). Teacher leadership teams: Choice, challenge, and change. Paper presented at the annual conference of the American Educational Research Association, San Diego, CA.

Deal, T. E., & Peterson, K. D. (1994). *The leadership paradox: Balancing logic and artistry in schools.* San Francisco, CA: JosseyBass Publishers.

Dimmock, C. (1999). Principals and school restructuring: Conceptualising challenges as dilemmas. *Journal of Educational Administration, 37*(5), 441–462.

Duffie, L. G. (1991). The principal: Leader or manager? Paper presented at the Annual Meeting of the Canadian Society for the Study of Education. ED339109.

Jenkins, B. (2009) "What it takes to be an instructional leader" *Principal, 88,* 34–37.

Kolb, D. A. (1984). *Experiential learning: Experience as the source of learning and development* (Vol. 1). Englewood Cliffs, NJ: Prentice-Hall.

Midgley, C., & Wood, S. (1993). Beyond site-based management: Empowering teachers to reform schools. *The Phi Delta Kappan, 75*(3), 245–252. Retrieved from http://www.jstor.org/stable/20405073

Peterson, K. (1994) *Building collaborative cultures: Seeking ways to reshape urban schools.* Urban Education Monograph Series. Naperville, IL: North Central Regional Education Laboratory.

Riggs, L. (2013). Great teachers don't always want to be principals. *The Atlantic.* Retrieved May 3, 2016, from https://www.theatlantic.com/education/archive/2013/11/great-teachers-dont-always-want-to-become-principals/281483/

Stronge, J. H. (1990). Managing for productive schools: The principal's role in contemporary education. *NASSP Bulletin,* March.

Stronge, J. H. (1993). Defining the principalship: Instructional leader or middle manager. *NASSP Bulletin,* May.

York-Barr, J., & Duke, K. (2004). What do we know about teacher leadership? Findings of two decades of scholarship. *Review of Educational Research, 74*(3), 255–316.

CHAPTER 7

Ash, R., & Persall, M. (2000). The principal as chief learning officer: Developing teacher leaders. *NASSP Bulletin, 84*(616), 15–22.

Barth, R. S. (2013). The time is ripe (again). *Educational Leadership, 71*(2). Retrieved from http://www.ascd.org/publications/educational-leadership/oct13/vol71/num02/The-Time-Is-Ripe-%28Again%29.aspx

Cuthbertson, J. (2014). How to become a teacher advocate. *Education Week Teacher,* Retrieved from http://www.edweek.org/tm/articles/2014/11/25/ctq-cuthbertson-teacer-advocate.html

Dewey, J. (1933). *How we think.* New York, NY: Prometheus Books.

Gehrke, N. (1991). Developing Teacher Leadership Skills. *ERIC Digest, ERIC: 5.*

Hargreaves, A. (1991). Contrived collegiality: The micropolitics of teacher collaboration. In J. Blase (Ed.), *The politics of life in schools* (pp. 46–72). New York, NY: Sage.

Harris, A., & Muijs, D. (2003). Teacher leadership and school improvement. *Education Review, 16*(2): 39–42.

Knight, J. (2007). *Instructional coaching.* Thousand Oaks, CA: Corwin Press.

Lambert, L. (2002). A framework for shared leadership. *Educational Leadership, 59*(8), 37–40.

Leithwood, K., & Jantzi, D. (2010). Principal and teacher leadership effects: A replication. *School Leadership and Management, 20*(4), 415–434.

Palmer, Parker J. (1998). The courage to teach: exploring the inner landscape of a teacher's life. San Francisco, CA: Jossey-Bass.

Sagor, R. (2000). *Guiding school improvement with action research.* Alexandria, VA: ASCD.

Schon, D. (1987). *Educating the reflective practitioner.* San Francisco, CA: Jossey-Bass.

Snell, J., & Swanson, J. (2000, April). The essential knowledge and skills of teacher leaders: A search for a conceptual framework. Paper presented at the annual meeting of the American Educational Research Association, New Orleans, LA.

Supovitz, J., & Christman, J. (2005) Small learning communities that actually learn: Lessons for school leaders. *Phi Delta Kappan, 86,* 649–651.

Zinn, L. F. (1997). Supports and barriers to teacher leadership: Reports on teacher leaders. Paper Presented at the annual meeting of the American Educational Research Association.

SUMMARY

Avolio, B. J., & Gardner, W. L. (2005). Authentic leadership development: Getting to the root of positive forms of leadership. *The Leadership Quarterly, 16,* 315–338.

Day, D. V., Zaccaro, S. J., & Halpin, S. M. (Ed.), (2004). *Leader development for transforming organizations: Growing leaders for tomorrow.* Mahwah, NJ: Erlbaum.

Gonzales, L. D. (2004). *Sustaining teacher leadership: Beyond the boundaries of enabling school culture.* Lanham, MD: University Press of America.

Kesler, G. C. (2002). Why the leadership bench never gets deeper: Ten insights about executive talent development. *Human Resource Planning* 25(1), 32–44.

About the Authors

Michael Coquyt, EdD, is currently an assistant professor of education at Minnesota State University Moorhead. He teaches primarily in the educational leadership graduate program. Coquyt also coordinates the curriculum and instruction graduate program. He has served as a superintendent, high school principal, and classroom teacher. He is the co-author of *The Leader Within: Understanding and Empowering Teacher Leaders*. Mike can be reached at michael.coquyt@mnstate.edu. He can also be found on Twitter at @MikeCoquyt.

Brian Creasman, EdD, is currently superintendent of Fleming County Schools in Kentucky. He has served as an assistant superintendent, a high school and middle school principal and assistant principal, and an instructional technologist and classroom teacher. He is the co-author of *The Leader Within: Understanding and Empowering Teacher Leaders*. Brian can be reached at briankcreasman@gmail.com. He can also be found on Twitter at @FCSSuper.